MW01030245

MORRIS ISLAND
AND THE
CIVIL WAR

MORRIS ISLAND
AND THE
CIVIL WAR

Strategy and Influence

C. RUSSELL HORRES JR.

THE
History
PRESS

Published by The History Press
Charleston, SC
www.historypress.com

Copyright © 2019 by C. Russell Horres Jr.
All rights reserved

First published 2019

Manufactured in the United States

ISBN 9781467141734

Library of Congress Control Number: 2018963666

Notice: The information in this book is true and complete to the best of our knowledge. It is offered without guarantee on the part of the author or The History Press. The author and The History Press disclaim all liability in connection with the use of this book.

All rights reserved. No part of this book may be reproduced or transmitted in any form whatsoever without prior written permission from the publisher except in the case of brief quotations embodied in critical articles and reviews.

CONTENTS

CONTENTS

ACKNOWLEDGEMENTS

I am grateful to all the historians and national park rangers with whom I have had the privilege of working over the many years that I have been involved in this project. They have all had a role in shaping this work. I also want to thank the librarians and archivists at the South Carolina Historical Society, the Charleston County Public Library, the Library of Congress, the National Archives, the Geisel Library at the University of California San Diego, the Wilson Library at the University of North Carolina, the South Caroliniana Library, the Coker College Library, the Charleston Library Society, the Fondren Library at Rice University and the Perkins Library at Duke University for their assistance in locating manuscripts and images.

A special appreciation is extended to professor emeritus Dr. Denis Brosnan at Clemson University, Major General Douglas Robertson (U.S. Army, retired) and John Turner Williamson, JD (U.S. Marine Corps, retired), who lent their expertise to reviewing this work.

I also am indebted to my family, who supported my efforts to understand what really happened on Morris Island during the Civil War.

INTRODUCTION

Fort Sumter's role in starting the Civil War was brief, relatively bloodless and front-page news. By contrast, in the final years of the conflict, the fort's role was prolonged, deadly and relegated to footnotes in news of the war despite the fact that the siege of the fort wore on for eighteen months and involved thousands of combatants on land and sea. That so much effort would be expended to capture Fort Sumter speaks not to its military importance but to its symbolic value. Fort Sumter became an icon of the war with opposite symbologies. To the North, Fort Sumter was where the rebellion began, the flag was attacked and the ignominy of defeat had to be avenged. To the South, the fort was the Lexington and Concord in the fight for Southern independence and had to be held at all cost. Visitors today are frequently astonished to find how small and insignificant the fort appears given its prominent role in starting the bloodiest war this nation has ever experienced.

The campaign for the fort lasted longer than the Sieges of Vicksburg and Petersburg combined, involved the personal intervention of President Abraham Lincoln and in the eyes of those directly involved produced very little of consequence either to the Union war efforts in the South Atlantic theater or to the Confederacy's promulgation of the war. However, in hindsight, through a most improbable sequence of events, what was accomplished, though unplanned, significantly changed the course of the war and the destiny of the nation. The contribution was not given its proper recognition, however, because it involved African Americans. Even today, many Americans do not appreciate the contributions African Americans made to the preservation of the Union and their own emancipation. A handful of leaders did understand the implications, but they were small voices in an arena with many competing views.

There are a number of conflicting accounts of what occurred during those eighteen months when men lived, fought and died on Morris Island—a narrow sandy island that is the nearest point of land to Fort Sumter. Some contemporary accounts no doubt were designed to obfuscate military objectives; others expressed racial biases prevalent in those times. Even more difficult to explain are reports of "eye witnesses" who could not have possibly observed close-quarter combat but reported on such as if they were involved. They were on the battleground, but they reconstructed events from hearsay, often from equally confused and frightened soldiers. Other events were twisted by history as a consequence of the inexactitude of reporting. One example that the author has encountered a number of times is history students who visit Fort Sumter convinced that Virginian Edmund Ruffin fired the first shot of the Civil War. "It must be true," they say, "I read it in a history book." The records show that Ruffin was on Morris Island on April 12, 1861, and was given the honor of firing the first shot at Fort Sumter from a particular battery on that island. Newspapers picked up the story, likely because Virginia had not yet determined to secede from the Union. If South Carolina and its six Southern colleagues were to have a chance at success, they needed Virginia in the fight. It was headline news that Ruffin had fired the first shot, but details of the actual sequence of firing on the fort by the various forts and batteries were omitted or only to be found by careful reading. Those records show that a number of shots had been fired in the early dawn by other batteries before Morris Island. Further, though Edmund Ruffin had indeed fired the first shot from his battery, a number of other batteries on Morris Island had fired before his. The headlines were repeated throughout the years as historian after historian recounted the events, so that over a century and a half later, readers are convinced it was Edmund Ruffin who started the Civil War.

In addition to the inexactitude of reporting in contributing to distorted accounts, military historians speak of the fog of war as confounding our ability to know what actually happens in battles. For example, the sequence that led to the firing on Fort Sumter was much like a clockwork mechanism, each event advancing toward conflict in irreversible steps. The meteoric rise of the Republican Party, which fused a nascent abolition movement into a political force; the divided election that made Abraham Lincoln president and triggered the secession of South Carolina; the dismissal of Fort Moultrie's commander and the appointment of Major Robert Anderson, the unit's second in command; and Anderson's decision to abandon Fort Moultrie for the safety of Fort Sumter all brought the start of war closer and closer. Anderson's move was seen by Southern leaders not as an effort to protect his garrison but as an act of war. Historians quickly realized how pivotal Anderson's decision to move the garrison was in setting the stage for the war but were confounded by the number of different views on when and how he evacuated Fort Moultrie that were prevalent only a decade after the events. Most of the participants, with the exception of Robert Anderson, were still alive at the time, and they were asked what happened. Their accounts differed markedly—the fog of war and fallibility of human memory had begun distorting our ability to know what actually happened the night after Christmas at Fort Moultrie in 1860. So it is with events on Morris Island later in the war—only there was much more going on than when the world was focused on Major Robert Anderson and his small garrison. Events at Vicksburg and Gettysburg were getting much more attention than events on Morris Island in the summer of 1863.

British historian E.H. Carr describes the facts of history not as fish lying in a market display but as fish swimming in a "vast and sometimes inaccessible ocean." The facts that you catch depend on factors such as chance but more importantly on what part of the ocean you fish in and what kind of net you use. The net used in this study of the Morris Island campaign and its results is one that attempts to strip away racial bias. Slavery ended in North America in 1867 when treaties with Native American tribes prohibited chattel slavery. The racial biases that allowed the practice to survive for nearly 250 years are so deeply ingrained in the American psyche that we continue to fight distorted perceptions. Historians were certainly not immune to them as they reflected on the Civil War. The perceptions that existed during the Civil War regarding African Americans would shock our modern sensibilities and were one of the greatest challenges this research faced. Is it possible to parse the truth from the biased views of the times? It indeed depends on the net that is used to sift the facts. This examination of the campaign seeks to better understand what trials African American troops faced during that campaign, how those trials were interpreted by their contemporaries and, more importantly, how perceptions were changed and, in turn, determined the progress of the war.

Any cursory reading on the campaign for Morris Island leaves one begging to know more about the nature of the defenses that the assaulting

Union forces encountered, for if you are to measure the success or failure of the campaign, you have to factor in the degree of difficulty of that effort. While there were a number of detached outposts on the island by the middle of 1863, the linchpin of the defenses was a massive earthwork that became known as Battery Wagner. The Confederate command dismissed it as a minor battery of little consequence; the Union saw it quite differently, elevating its status to a fortification. Could a minor battery have stalled the efforts of a determined army supported by the best technology the U.S. Navy had to offer? This work attempts to resolve the two views by examining the battery's component parts, how it utilized natural barriers and the effort involved in withstanding two major land assaults and over sixty days of artillery barrages from land and sea that at times were so intense that an observer described the earthwork as an erupting volcano.

It can be argued that efforts to capture Battery Wagner were misdirected and the strength of the objective unimportant because it singularly failed to do what it was designed to do: protect Fort Sumter from land-based artillery. Fort Sumter was destroyed by long-range artillery fire while Wagner held the northern third of the island. Then the Confederates abandoned Wagner—no longer needed to protect the iconic fort—and the entire island to the Union forces. History shows that the two failed assaults, massive bombardments and miles of trench works against Wagner were unnecessary. Certainly the determined and costly resistance by the Confederates at Battery Wagner delayed the demise of the iconic Fort Sumter and gave time to prepare a new line of defense, but what did assaulting it accomplish short of establishing a good case for calling it a fort instead of a battery? At issue is not the flawed strategy but what was demanded of men sent to capture the battery: not individual bravery, of which there were many stellar examples, but the collective bravery of a regiment of black men called to be soldiers in the Union army. Men with no rights of citizenship, resented by all, who were willing to die to make this country a better place for their race. Were these men brave or were they mere mortals who ran away from the fight, as some would attest? Much of that answer is embedded in how they were sent into battle and what they faced on Morris Island.

As a defensive barrier for Charleston, the island itself could not have been better designed. The entrance to Charleston Harbor is flanked to the north by Sullivan's Island and to the south by Morris Island. Fort Sumter stood on a man-made island between the two. One of a chain of barrier islands along the South Carolina coast, Morris Island was at the beginning of the Civil War approximately 3⅔ miles in length and 1,200 yards at its widest point. The island was marked by a number of substantial sand dunes, some reaching 36 feet in height, tall enough to be called hills. These natural elevations provided places where detached gun batteries could be emplaced.

A connection with Charleston Harbor was open to shallow-draft vessels for about half of Morris Island's northern extension via Vincent's Creek, now over-washed and filled with sand. The end of the island nearest Fort Sumter curved westward toward Charleston and was known as Cummings Point. Here only ¾ of a mile of open water separated Fort Sumter from its southern neighbor. Small vessels from the harbor could also land at the point. The main shipping channel from Charleston Harbor turned to the south just past Fort Sumter and ran about a mile offshore along the entire length of Morris Island before entering the Atlantic. Since the late 1600s, a series of lights and lighthouses had been built on the southern end of Morris Island to mark the entrance from the Atlantic. The federal government built a brick lighthouse in the 1830s that stood over 100 feet above the ocean and operated it until it was demolished by the Confederates. The southern end of the island was divided from Little Folly Island by a passage 345 yards wide. The inlet was too deep to ford but impassable to deep-draft vessels. In addition to the lighthouse, only a few structures stood on the island before the war. Most notable was a substantial house built in 1856 by Captain George Cullum, then chief engineer working on Fort Sumter. This frame house on a raised brick foundation was about midway between Cummings Point and the lighthouse. Known as the Beacon House, it was designed as the dwelling for the lightkeeper and his family.[1] Unlike the lighthouse, which was destroyed early in the war, the Beacon House was a prominent landmark during the campaign.

Once on the island, in addition to the surrounding waters, nature presents a most formidable obstacle to going further toward Charleston. Separating the island from the mainland are nearly two and a half miles of coastal salt marsh laced with networks of narrow tidal creeks. All of this is much too shallow for gunboats to operate in and muddy and deep enough to prevent troops from passing over it. During the campaign, a Union lieutenant was ordered to construct a gun battery in the marsh behind Morris Island from which the city could be bombarded—he commented that he would comply but had to requisition eighteen-foot-tall men. His commanding officer understood his point but did not appreciate his sarcasm.[2] The solution to successfully building a gun platform on this quagmire was ingenious.

Its remoteness and geography gave the island its other useful occupation in the years before the war. About three-quarters of a mile south of Cummings

Point at a point accessible to the inner harbor via Vincent's Creek stood a cluster of six buildings, including a lazaretto or quarantine hospital, dock and boathouse.[3] With little that medicine could do at the time to cure often-fatal diseases such as yellow fever and smallpox, the quarantine station was equipped with the obligatory graveyard. This area was near the site chosen to build the island's major defensive work. Soldiers attempting to approach Battery Wagner with trench work recounted the unpleasantness of disinterring corpses while trenching through the graveyard.

Sketches made by Captain Truman Seymour of the Fort Sumter garrison shortly before the war show the island covered with low trees and vegetation. Later in the war, it would be practically stripped bare of anything that blocked a view or could be of value in camp. With salt water surrounding the island, it is remarkable that trees could grow in the sandy soil. The presence of large trees points to an unexpected source of fresh water. As soldiers discovered when building camps on the island, several feet beneath the island's sand was a thin layer of potable water provided by rain falling on the dunes. Digging a deeper well only resulted in salt water, as one would expect being so close to the ocean. The fresh water, lower in density than the underlying salt water, floats on top. The sand prevents the fresh water from mixing with the salt water. Diffusion, a process that over a long period of time would distribute the salt equally into the freshwater layer, is so slow that as long as the rain continues to replenish it, a supply of fresh water is available. Unfortunately, as soldiers learned during the war, this meager supply was easily contaminated.

Coastal geologists tell us that the barrier islands off the coast of South Carolina have been moving westward toward the mainland since the end of the last ice age almost 18,000 years ago, when ocean levels were hundreds of feet lower than at present. The shoreline then was almost forty miles east of its present position. The changes to Morris Island in the last 158 years have been dramatic, and the island is classified as unsuitable for development. Erosion has been exacerbated by jetties built to change the channel into Charleston Harbor.[4] None of the trench works or the batteries built on the main part of the island during the Civil War have survived the erosion of the island. The northern end was threatened by development in 2006, and the Trust for Public Lands mounted a fund-raising campaign that resulted in the threatened property being transferred to the City of Charleston for permanent protection.

These natural and man-made alterations to Morris Island make any study of the campaign dependent on historical charts and maps. There are no remains of Battery Wagner save the beach sand that covers the footprint of what would have been its west-facing parapet. Though Cummings Point remains in its approximate Civil War position, storms are constantly reshaping it, and none of the extensive Civil War landmarks remain. There are two historical renderings that are of particular importance to appreciating the island and its structures during the war. The first was done by an artist, William Aiken Walker, who served with the Confederate engineers at Charleston as a draftsman and cartographer. Walker shows every detail of the sand hills and creeks of the island with an artist's eye. The second is a rendering of Battery Wagner done under the auspices of Confederate engineer Francis D. Lee that shows the line of the original open battery before it was ordered to be modified into a powerful fortification. Until this drawing was found, there was no way to discern what was originally planned for Morris Island's defense. Both of these illustrations are included for the reader's reference (on pages 66 and 65, respectively).

Just as the island itself is in motion, one cannot omit the fact that defensive and offensive works on the island were not static. As the probing artillery revealed weaknesses, the engineers would design new defenses. It would be a serious error to use the plans drawn by Union engineers after the Confederates evacuated as representative of the battery when first assaulted almost two months earlier. What is instructive about the after-action plans is how well the structure resisted relentless artillery bombardment from land and sea. This fact made an indelible impression upon Admiral John Dahlgren, inventor of the Dahlgren naval gun. He realized how ineffective his guns were against the earthwork. This observation did not go unnoticed by Confederate general Pierre Gustave Toutant Beauregard, who proceeded to line Charleston's inner harbor with similar earth batteries. To fully grasp the work that was done during the siege day by day requires a careful reading of the *Official Records of the War of the Rebellion*. As the campaign was a combined effort, both the army and navy records contain details of the account.

Changing technology also had a role in the campaign. As it geared up to defend itself, South Carolina received the gift of a remarkable innovation in cannon design that employed the concept of rifling the weapon's barrel to impart a spin to the projectile as it exited the cannon. The spin stabilized the projectile in flight, dramatically improving accuracy. This novel rifled cannon was placed at Cummings Point on Morris Island in 1861 only three-quarters of a mile from the southwest corner of Fort Sumter. The cannon was so accurate that the Confederates were able to target the two-foot-by-three-foot openings of Fort Sumter's embrasures. A number of projectiles passed through the narrow openings. The accuracy of this rifled cannon was unparalleled, and its abilities were noted by both sides of the battle for Fort Sumter. Observant artillerymen even carried the small Blakely shells back to the North when they evacuated.

The rush was on to produce even larger-caliber rifled artillery. Britain continued its pioneering work, but both the Union and the Confederacy were soon in the game, and by the start of the campaign for Morris Island, both sides had large-caliber rifled artillery. The Union brought seven-, eight- and ten-inch versions to Morris Island. The South, though more limited in manufacturing capabilities, could by 1862 both design and build large-caliber rifles and modify existing smoothbores by machining groves into their barrels and adding reinforcing bands to accommodate the higher pressures required for the heavier projectiles. Some British seacoast rifles were also obtained through the less-than-perfect Union blockade. Fort Sumter had two excellent seven-inch Brooke rifles that could reach Light House Inlet from the fort, a distance of almost five miles. Later, military historians would recount that "modern artillery" was introduced to warfare at Morris Island. The range of the rifled artillery exceeded the ability of the eye to see the point of impact, and the first recorded use of compass-directed artillery fire was from Morris Island at the city of Charleston during the campaign.

Artillery innovations were closely followed by the development of ironclad ships that could operate in close support of the troops on the island. Mounting massive fifteen-inch smoothbore guns, the ironclads became adept at bouncing their massive explosive projectiles into Battery Wagner. Another notable use of technology was the searchlight. Though developed for the stage productions, the so-called limelights played an important role in the campaign. The hydrogen-powered Drummond lights were employed to illuminate the Confederate fortifications from miles away, thwarting efforts to repair the forts under the cover of darkness. Producing the gas for the lights and storing it in bladders on Morris Island was no mean feat. By the 1860s, telegraphy was well developed, as were Daniell cells for chemically producing electricity. It was not a huge leap to realize that one could use electricity passing through rubber-insulated wires to remotely detonate underwater mines. At the first attempt by the U.S. Navy to capture Fort Sumter in April 1863, the navy's latest battleship, the *New Ironsides*, inadvertently sat over a two-thousand-pound mine while technicians at Battery Wagner attempted to detonate the mine. For reasons not entirely known, they were not able to ignite the fuse. Had that innovation worked and the grand warship been destroyed, the campaign for Morris Island would be an entirely different story. As it was, the combined efforts of artillery from Fort Sumter and Fort Moultrie, located a mile to the north, gave the ironclad fleet a significant battering, caused the navy to rethink the importance of its iron ships and setting the stage for the campaign for Morris Island.

Finally, this story is about linkages that have roots in the events that shaped the struggle for a tiny spit of sand. Those events did not happen in a vacuum, so this work may seem to digress at points, but connections that initially seem obtuse will fall into place once the full spectrum is revealed. One might wonder for example how General Beauregard's success at far-away Manassas, Virginia; Robert E. Lee's assignments early in the war; or Abraham Lincoln's Emancipation Proclamation could possibly have a connection to the events on Morris Island, but they did, and in time, those linkages will become clear.

Chapter 1

MORRIS ISLAND AT THE START
OF THE CIVIL WAR

How Fort Sumter came to be associated with the start of the Civil War is as convoluted as the causes of the war itself. Although you can point to the mortar shell that exploded over the fort in the predawn hours of April 12, 1861, as the beginning, events conspired over months and years to bring the nation to the brink of war. Even after the bombardment, some optimistic souls concluded that South Carolina had only acquired what rightfully belonged to it, and since there were no reported deaths, the matter should be considered concluded.[5] After all, had not emissaries of the newly seceded Republic of South Carolina offered to purchase the incomplete fortification? Shouldn't the federal government, with its vast resources, just let Fort Sumter go as it had other Southern forts and arsenals? But there was no room for optimism; the South had made a fatal mistake in appealing to violence, precisely fitting President Abraham Lincoln's objectives. The bombardment had been silenced hardly a day and Anderson was still packing to leave Fort Sumter when telegrams that assured a state of war were sent from Washington. Addressed to state governors, the telegrams called up a seventy-five-thousand-man army to put down the rebellion with details already prepared for muster points for the individual regiments. Powerless under the Constitution to prevent secession, Lincoln knew that rebellion would enable him to raise an army to suppress it, allow him to invade states in rebellion and hence put an end to secession and its dire consequences for the untested Union.

States North and South had long flirted with the concept of secession as they chafed under federal laws and tariffs they felt unjust. One of the earliest predictors of a fracture along the Mason-Dixon Line was Vice President John C. Calhoun. The nation's beginnings were deeply rooted in agriculture and forest products. Early wealth and power were derived from agricultural products, but change was in the wind in the form of the Industrial Revolution that had transformed Europe. The South had pushed its economy into an expanding slave-based agricultural system, while the North, with its capital not tied up in slaves, could pursue industrialization. For the first forty years under the U.S. Constitution, agricultural wealth controlled the government. However, in 1828, Northern industrial wealth tilted the powerbase and succeeded in passing a punitive tariff on the South's agricultural products. Vice President Calhoun saw this as the beginning of sectionalism, with no end but for the nation to divide along economic lines.[6] Calhoun did not live to see it happen, but his vision was correct. With the election of Lincoln as the precipitating event and the right of the state to protect slavery against federal intervention an underlying cause, South Carolina and six other Southern states put theory to test and voted themselves out of the Union. Although Lincoln recognized the right of Americans to overthrow a government they felt weary of, he believed that the concerns expressed by the South were not just cause to do so. He pointed to the constitutional amendment being ratified to prevent the federal government from ever interfering with a state's internal institutions, including that of persons held to service, and the federal law mandating the return of fugitive slaves to their owners.[7]

A more vexing question is why Lincoln felt compelled to reinforce Fort Sumter at that particular time. While Major Anderson and his garrison were low on supplies, it can hardly be said that they were starving. Records indicate that the garrison was permitted to purchase fresh meat and vegetables from Charleston markets. Because they were prohibited from entering the city for fear of an incident with the citizens, their supplies were delivered to nearby Fort Johnson along with the mail.[8] This arrangement ended when Lincoln informed South Carolina governor Francis Pickens that he would reinforce his fort peacefully or by force if necessary. Further, the stalemate at Fort Sumter was already in its fourth month, and the Charleston defenses were well advanced. Given the failed relief attempt by the *Star of the West* in January, when only a few hastily erected batteries opposed it, surely the time had passed for a successful coup de main.

The federal government had already walked away from a number of arsenals, post offices, courthouses, customhouses and fortifications in other seceded states. Only at Fort Sumter and Fort Pickens in Florida were U.S. troops resisting evacuation. Would two more forts matter? Of Lincoln's cabinet, only Postmaster General Montgomery Blair believed that Fort Sumter should be provisioned and relieved with new soldiers and proposed a plan by his son-in-law, Captain Gustavus Fox, to do so.[9] To do less, in Blair's opinion, would be an admission of weakness for the administration. Successful or not, he felt the attempt would be a sign of the administration's resolve to do something about secession and would inspire loyal Southerners to rise up against the traitors.[10] As William Porter Alexander posited in his memoir of the war, of what value could Fort Sumter be to the Northern states if not to subject South Carolina to Northern control? Lincoln could have waited and appealed to negotiation. In a Union of thirty-three states, only seven had resorted to secession, and they were in the Deep South.

A clue as to why Lincoln acted soon after taking office may be found in the attitudes of New Yorkers. New York papers were full of approbation for South Carolina's secession in December 1860. New York business interests saw secession as good for business. That was until March, when they learned the full impact of the Morrill tariff plan that the Republican Party wanted to initiate to increase federal revenue. It became clear that the new tariffs would apply solely to states remaining in the Union and not to the seceded states, which were free to establish their own tariffs and thereby put New York traders at a distinct disadvantage. Attitudes in the Empire State changed abruptly against secession. There was another pressing issue that was less hypothetical. Federal revenues depended in large part on the customs duties levied at Southern ports. With their secession, South Carolina, Georgia, Florida, Alabama, Louisiana, Mississippi and Texas were not collecting the needed revenues. It hardly seems an issue today, but after the War of 1812, the nation actually generated budget surpluses. However, by 1858, the nation had begun to run deficits, and without the revenue from the Southern states, the situation was dire. The political turmoil of secession made financing the debt unfavorable. Lincoln had inherited not only a divided nation but also a nation in financial extremis. He was under pressure to do something about secession, and he had two options—Fort Sumter or Fort Pickens. He chose both.

It was only by a comedy of errors that the Civil War did not start at Fort Pickens. The president's wish that reinforcements already on ships anchored near Fort Pickens be landed were opposed by the local commander, who believed a "gentlemen's agreement" with Confederate forces prevented him from doing so. By the time a second messenger was sent to inform the commander that the president was under no such obligation, events at Charleston began to unfold. Lincoln was intimately involved in the planning, interviewing and assigning subordinates and bypassing the secretary of the navy, Gideon Welles, and army general Winfield Scott, both of whom opposed the plan. Orders became crossed up, and a warship essential for the success of the Fort Sumter mission got sent to Pensacola, where it was not needed.

It is ironic that a fort designed to protect America from the humiliation of foreign invasion, as occurred during the War of 1812, should be the flashpoint in a civil war. But there is much about Fort Sumter that is atypical. As part of the third system of fortifications designed to protect coastal cities, Fort Sumter was problematic from the very beginning. When it was conceived, the effective range of heavy artillery was not much over a mile. Cannons, if elevated, could send projectiles farther but lacked accuracy. Two earlier Charleston fortifications proved the weakness of being more than a mile apart in the Revolutionary War. The palmetto-log-and-sand fortification that would come to be known as Fort Moultrie, built at the start of that war on Sullivan's Island on the north side of Charleston Harbor, could not be helped by Fort Johnson, located almost two and a half miles to the southwest on James Island. The ideal spot from the point view of artillery was about one mile from both of the existing forts. Unfortunately, there was no dry land at that location, only a narrow shoal in the harbor consisting of consecutive layers of sand and mud about sixty-five feet deep sitting on top of the more compacted marl—marine sediment that underlies the Charleston area to a depth of nearly two thousand feet. The sand and silt were far too deep for the pile driving of the day, so the engineers gambled and decided on a spread foundation of granite rocks. The limitations of overland transportation necessitated shipping the granite from the Northeast, where it could be loaded on ships from seaside quarries and brought to Charleston. Once in port, the granite could be offloaded onto barges, from which enslaved workers could manually push the large blocks into the harbor. Construction began in 1829 on the new "three tiered battery opposite Fort Moultrie,"[11] with the Corps of Engineers placing buoys and marking off an irregular pentagon with measuring chains and poles. The laborious process continued for eleven years until the granite was at nine feet above mean low sea level, about three feet above the normal high tide. When contrasted with third-system forts built on dry land that could typically be completed in thirteen years, spending eleven years just to build a foundation was a very slow process. While this was going on, South Carolina decided to tweak the federal government by announcing that the harbor bottom where the fort was being built was claimed by the state comptroller general, William Laval. This further added to the delay in building the fort until those claims could be invalidated. Adding to the slowness was the perception that the climate in South Carolina was unhealthy in the summer months, when workmen left the site. By 1840, the fort's wharf was complete and could be used to temporarily store millions of handmade bricks as they were distributed around the pentagon to raise the walls. Contrary to popular belief, Fort Sumter's walls are not solid brick but are actually a thick veneer of brick enclosing an interlocking concrete core. The embrasures, openings through which the cannons fired, are surrounded by an even stronger material, an artificial stone formed in molds by pounding a mixture of cement, small pieces of brick rubble, crushed oyster shells, sand and water. These strong blocks were covered on the interior by decorative carved brownstone surrounds.

The design of the fort placed its primary defensive capability on its faces and flank walls. The pentagon was oriented so that the face to the right of the salient or point was parallel to Fort Moultrie to assure that enemy ships entering the harbor would have to run a gauntlet well within the range of both forts. The rear or gorge wall, facing Morris Island just three-quarters of a mile to the south, was only lightly armed and contained the primary entrance or sally port of the fort and its landing wharf. An artillery siege from that direction was simply not anticipated, and the fort's two-story powder magazines were located in the east and west corners of the gorge wall. Although its weakness from the rear was revealed during the Civil War, the third-system fort designers viewed the fortification as only a temporary impediment to foreign invasion. The primary mode of defense would be a strong navy and a standing army that could be quickly concentrated at points of attack. The planners viewed two weeks as adequate to bring forward reinforcements, and magazines and food and water stores were based on that requirement.

The gorge wall was not Fort Sumter's only weakness. When the fort's walls reached their intended height of forty-three feet above the foundation, it was realized that the mud and silt of the shoal could not support the massive weight. Measurements referenced to an iron pipe driven deep in the sand and mud began to indicate that the walls were subsiding. The casemate structures immediately behind the outer walls were not attached to the walls but were actually free-standing structures that did not have the mass of the outer walls. This created a concern about setting the floor levels of the second of the three tiers and resulted in even more delay in construction to wait until the annual subsidence stopped. While the casemates awaited completion, the engineers worked on the barracks and quarters for a peacetime garrison of about 565 officers and men. In times of war, this number could swell to nearly 750 soldiers.

The fall of 1860 saw a press to complete the work, not because anyone thought a civil war was eminent but because of the possibility of foreign intervention in our troubled relations with Mexico. The workforce in the fall of 1860 was almost doubled, and all of the second-tier casemate vaults were completed, along with planned improvements at Fort Moultrie across the channel. After twenty-nine years under construction, the fort was finally edging toward completion. Cannons and ammunition had been purchased and stored on site. The magazines were complete and contained over thirty-nine thousand pounds of coarsely milled cannon powder under the protection of their thick walls equipped with lightning rods.[12] The embrasures for the second tier remained to be completed. In the fall of 1860, they were large, square openings awaiting installation of newly designed cast-iron Totten shutters, which would open and close with the operation of the cannons, thereby preventing enemy fire from entering the casemate. New Hampshire–born Captain John G. Foster, the superintending engineer in the final years before the war, had a large number of these plates and the three-hundred-pound solid iron jamb posts to which they were to be hinged on hand. They would come in handy preparing the fort for attack. Another missing item was the huge iron portcullis, which was designed to be lowered to close the sally port in times of threat. Although it was completed, delivery had been delayed by a severe freeze on the Hudson River the previous winter. On a brighter note, the water collection and distribution systems were working, and the enlisted men's barracks and elaborate officer's quarters were finished. Officers could enjoy the luxury of having hot and cold running water. The kitchen chimneys had been embedded with lead water pipes fed from cast-iron storage tanks in the attics of the quarters to act as water heaters. To collect rainwater, terra-cotta pipes channeled water that had been cleaned by filtering through beds of sand high on the parapets into cisterns under the floors of the casemates. Manual pumps were used to transport water from the cisterns to the attic reservoir tanks. Each cistern held about five thousand gallons, and there was a cistern in the middle of each face.

Such was the state of Fort Sumter when Major Robert Anderson decided to relocate his small garrison of artillerists from Fort Moultrie to the imposing fort in the middle of the mouth of Charleston Harbor. His clandestine arrival in the middle of the night created a stir among the throngs of workmen who resided at the fort, many sympathetic to the South and the rising calls for secession. In abandoning Fort Moultrie on the night after Christmas, Anderson ordered its cannons to be disabled and its flagpole cut down, creating the impression that he had been ordered to do so by higher authorities. His move certainly perturbed Secretary of War John Floyd, who immediately telegrammed him to return to his post at Fort Moultrie. Sympathetic to the South, Secretary Floyd, under suspicion of fraud, resigned when President Buchanan refused to order Anderson to withdraw from Fort Sumter.

Only two months earlier, Anderson, second in command of the First Artillery, had been on temporary assignment in New York before being ordered to replace Colonel John L. Gardner, his sixty-seven-year-old superior officer at Fort Moultrie, whom the army felt due to his advanced age and temperament was ill-suited to dealing with the political volatility in Charleston arising from the election of Abraham Lincoln on November 8, 1860. The agrarian South had been losing political power to the rapidly industrializing North for decades, and its embrace of the practice of chattel slavery stood in sharp contradistinction to the sentiments of eighteen northern and midwestern states that had independently abolished the reviled institution. The Republican Party, formed in 1856 on an antislavery platform, capitalized on a split in the dominant Democratic Party over slavery and won the presidential election in just four short years. South Carolina vowed that the election of Lincoln would result in secession. The U.S. Army at Charleston was in a delicate position. As the most visible evidence of federal authority and charged with protection of federal properties in the state, it no doubt felt the enmity of the citizens.

Arriving in Charleston in mid-November, Major Anderson quickly realized that the men in his command, numbering less than eighty, were inadequate to the mission of protecting the four harbor forts—Johnson, Sumter, Moultrie and Castle Pinckney—under his control. His predecessor had called for immediate reinforcement and found himself on the way to a remote outpost command in San Antonio, Texas. Anderson, seeing the abundant number of workmen under the charge of Captain Foster, came up with a scheme to arm them with muskets and encouraged Foster to draw the weapons from the federal arsenal in Charleston. Foster sent a contingent of men to do just that and was met with considerable anger from alert citizens who telegraphed the secretary of war about the removal of forty smoothbore muskets from the arsenal. Secretary Floyd immediately telegraphed Captain Foster ordering him to return the muskets. By this incident, Major Anderson had to know that he was there only to maintain the status quo.

Anderson's headquarters at Fort Moultrie were not an isolated post. The low fort sat in the middle of a beach vacation spot for Charlestonians. The Atlantic House, a resort hotel, stood just north of the post. Nearby houses actually looked down into the fort. Contact with local citizens was unavoidable, and no doubt the tension was palpable as South Carolina drew closer to seceding from the Union. True to their word, within weeks of learning the election results, a secession convention was called for at noon on December 17 at the First Baptist Church in Columbia, the largest building in the capital city at that time. The next day, the convention withdrew from the state capital in Columbia to Charleston because of a rumored smallpox epidemic and reconvened at the Institute Hall on Meeting Street, next to the Circular Congregationalist Church. The next day, it began closed-door sessions at the St. Andrew's Hall on Broad Street, and on the nineteenth, it approved the ordinance of secession without a dissenting vote. That evening, the delegates paraded from the St. Andrew's Hall to the Institute Hall, where before a capacity crowd of nearly three thousand jubilant onlookers, they formally signed the ordinance, becoming the independent Republic of South Carolina. The emotional outpouring was astounding, and the celebrations continued for days. Only the approach of Christmas cooled the ardor. With militia units marching through the city, Anderson felt his position at Fort Moultrie untenable, and without counsel of the war department or of his subordinate officers, he determined to move the garrison—a move that would almost assure Fort Sumter's role in the coming conflict.[13]

On his arrival at the fort under cover of darkness, he arranged for Captain Foster to discharge workers who would not swear allegiance to the federal government and began to prepare the fort for the attack he felt almost certain would come. His island outpost at Castle Pinckney, close by the city, was commandeered the next day by an overwhelming force of South Carolina militia, followed by occupation of the abandoned Forts Moultrie and Johnson. In short order, the strategic position occupied by Morris Island was recognized by the state. In his January 6 report to Colonel Samuel Cooper, Anderson noted that the South Carolinians were busy erecting batteries bearing on the harbor entrance.[14]

Morris Island was ideally positioned for its coming role. The closest land position to Fort Sumter, aligned with the fort's most vulnerable wall, made it the perfect position from which to bombard the fort. In addition, with ships in the main channel exposed broadside for almost the entire length of the island, it was a perfect position to control access to Fort Sumter and the inner harbor. Lookouts stationed on the south end of the island could provide warning of ships attempting to cross the bar.

While local and state militia units were busy occupying Castle Pinckney and repairing Fort Moultrie, newly elected governor Francis Pickens sensed the importance of Morris Island and drew on a reserve that had connections to the fears of slave resurrection that haunted antebellum society. Chasing wealth generated by plantation-based agricultural products, primarily rice and cotton, had placed the state in a position where enslaved blacks outnumbered whites. Chattel slavery in the South depended on inculcated fear amplified by brutal examples of the consequences of disobedience, strict regulation on freedom of movement and a police state exemplified by night patrols with authority to shoot to kill. The possibility of rebellion was real, and though earlier rebellions in South Carolina were quickly suppressed, the successful violent rebellion in Santo Domingo around 1800 illustrated all too well what could happen in South Carolina. In 1822, a loyal slave alerted authorities that Denmark Vesey, a fifty-five-year-old free black carpenter, was planning a revolt possibly involving thousands of slaves in Charleston and on neighboring plantations. Vesey and about 30 others thought to be involved were publicly executed. Authorities realized that a rebellion of that size would overwhelm city police and local slave patrols and petitioned the state government to establish arsenals where arms could be stored to enable a rapid response to any uprising. An act was passed that year authorizing the building of an arsenal in the area of Marion Square and the organization of a standing army to be known as the Municipal Guard. Ten years later, the term "citadel" was used in a funding act for the state arsenal at Charleston. Columbia had its own arsenal, the officers' quarters of which is now the Governor's Mansion. In 1842, the citadel at Charleston and the arsenal in Columbia were both converted to military schools subsequently known as the Citadel Academy and Arsenal Academy at Columbia. When the two schools were combined into the South Carolina Military Academy in January 1861 and formed into a battalion of state cadets, they numbered about 170 students. Although accounts vary on the dates, by December 31, Governor Pickens notes that he ordered a contingent of about 50 cadets from the Citadel Academy under superintendent Major Peter Fayssoux Stevens to hastily prepare a battery of twenty-four pounders in the sand dunes near the old quarantine hospital on Morris Island.

The position was out of the range of Fort Sumter's guns and was shielded from view from the fort by the intervening sand dunes. More importantly, it bore directly on the main shipping channel. For protection, the battery was revetted with sandbags. Accounts differ as to how many guns the battery mounted—some say three, others four. Compared to the heavy seacoast cannons of Fort Sumter and Fort Moultrie, the twenty-four-pounder siege cannon was a relatively light weapon that could be operated off of a wheeled field carriage. It threw a 5.75-inch-diameter, twenty-four-pound ball accurately out to about a mile with an eight-pound charge of coarse cannon powder. It was not long before the battery would see action.

Sensing that Major Anderson had gotten himself in a predicament, President Buchanan responded quickly and ordered a relief expedition. A commercial two-masted sidewheel steamer, the *Star of the West*, was chartered and two hundred hand-picked men were secretly boarded with extra arms, ammunition and provisions and given orders to conceal themselves below deck when approaching Fort Sumter. The steamship reached Charleston on January 9, crossed the bar and proceeded up the shipping channel until it came in range of the cadets' battery at about 7:15 a.m. The cadets fired a warning shot across the ship's bow, but it defiantly raised a large U.S. flag and continued on. As it continued to draw within range of Fort Moultrie, Major Roswell Ripley ordered a ten-inch Columbiad bearing on the channel to open fire, but the gun fell short. A second shot from the Morris Island battery fell astern, but the third shot from the cadets hit the ship in the hull. At that, the *Star of the West* ended its relief expedition. As it retreated, more shots were fired from Morris Island. The Charleston *Courier* the next day reported that a total of seventeen shots were fired, including three from Moultrie that fell short. Major Anderson's garrison, observing the entire scene from their guns, were ready to return fire, but calmer heads prevailed, and nothing more than an exchange of indignant letters occurred. Anecdotally, Captain Abner Doubleday claimed that he had to restrain one of the garrison's wives, outraged at the insult to the U.S. flag, from pulling a lanyard. Although his account cannot be verified, it is known that when the garrison moved to Fort Sumter, about forty-nine women and children from the Moultrie community came with them. They would be evacuated in early February to New York. If anything, the shots fired telegraphed a message that the Republic of South Carolina was taking its sovereignty seriously.

The *Star of the West* incident has an interesting legacy. The *Star* itself was captured by Galveston, Texas militia two months later and served the Confederacy until it was scuttled in the Tallahatchie River in front of Fort

Pemberton to block a U.S. flotilla from reaching Vicksburg in 1863. The fort was named for Lieutenant General John C. Pemberton, who will be remembered for his troubles at Charleston and the surrender of an entire Confederate army at Vicksburg. The Citadel cadets who fired on the *Star* became legendary as having fired the first shots of the Civil War. Generations of Citadel graduates have learned that cadet corporal George Edward Haynsworth pulled the lanyard on the warning shot across the ship's bow. Haynsworth, a Sumter, South Carolina native, was a senior at the Citadel Academy and would serve in the Confederate army in the First South Carolina Artillery, a unit that witnessed much of the struggle for Morris Island. Though he survived the war and participated with his unit in the last major engagement in the East, the Battle of Bentonville, North Carolina, he was mortally wounded in a shootout between feuding clans in his Sumter law offices in 1887. Though there is some merit to the Citadel's claims, the incident was one of a series leading to the battle that clearly started the war. Governor Pickens and others felt that Robert Anderson's disabling of Fort Moultrie's guns and clandestine move to Fort Sumter were acts of war.

Twelve days following the *Star of the West* incident, Major Anderson reported to the secretary of war that the South Carolinians were constructing batteries several hundred yards south of the Citadel's battery and that workmen had been active for about a week building an extensive series of batteries on Cummings Point, the westward-curving northernmost extremity of Morris Island. What evolved from this work over the next few months were three batteries. The Cummings Point Battery mounted three ten-inch mortars for high-arcing fire over the fort's walls and two twenty-four pounders to aim low-trajectory direct fire. Next to the Cummings Point Battery was the Stevens Ironclad Battery, mounting three eight-inch Columbiads in a design reflecting the protective concept of Fort Sumter's casemates. This battery was built to direct fire at Fort Sumter from behind an iron shield. The sloped timber battery was covered with railroad tracks, and its embrasures were protected by heavy iron shutters operated by a lever. Its designer, Clement Hoffman Stevens, had been involved in railroad construction before the war. He distinguished himself as an infantry commander and was killed in the Battle of Atlanta in 1864. The Stevens Ironclad Battery was followed by the Trapier Battery, mounting three eight-inch Columbiads and three ten-inch mortars behind a sturdy timber-and-sandbag parapet. Stevens's ironclad battery was not the only one being prepared to put Fort Sumter under siege. A more radical design was in the works on the Charleston waterfront. Former U.S. Navy lieutenant John R.

Lieutenant Truman Seymour on Major Anderson's staff rendered the South Carolina military activities on Morris Island on February 13, 1861. *From* The War of the Rebellion: Atlas to Accompany the Official Records *(Washington, D.C.: Government Printing Office, 1895).*

Hamilton Jr. had begun converting a large barge into a four-gun floating battery with a sloping parapet covered in railroad rails and boiler plate. Though considered a folly by some, the concept would prove itself viable in the coming battle. Beauregard had it towed to the west end of Sullivan's Island, where it could enfilade the left flank of Fort Sumter.[15]

Except for a few outspoken radicals like Robert Barnwell Rhett, South Carolina's scheme in seceding was not to go it alone. The state viewed the immediate precipitating factor for secession as the election of Abraham Lincoln and the ascendency of the Republican Party, which threatened the institution of slavery around which Southern life revolved. Along with its "Causes of Secession," the South Carolina Secession Convention issued a call to slaveholding states urging them to join South Carolina in a Southern confederacy. On January 2, South Carolina elected commissioners to each of the Southern states that had called for a secession convention.[16] On the day the *Star of the West* was fired on, Mississippi seceded, followed by Florida, Alabama, Georgia and Louisiana. On February 1, Texas became the seventh to secede. The plan was working. South Carolina ceased to be an independent republic on February 8, when the first six states met in Montgomery, Alabama, to adopt a provisional constitution. Former U.S. senator Jefferson Davis was elected president and inaugurated on February 15. Charleston's problems with Major Anderson would now become the Confederacy's.

On March 3, Charleston was introduced to Pierre Gustave Toutant Beauregard. A career army officer from Louisiana whose appointment as commandant of the U.S. Military Academy at West Point was withdrawn when Louisiana seceded only five days after he assumed the position, Beauregard was appointed as the Confederacy's first brigadier general on March 1. He was promptly ordered to Charleston, where he arrived two days later and set up headquarters in the Charleston Hotel. The very next day, he inspected the defenses that the South Carolinians had been preparing for two months. He was not pleased with what he saw. The work on Fort Moultrie he found particularly deficient and ordered it torn down and rebuilt. On Morris Island, he immediately saw a mistake in the concentration of batteries on Cummings Point. He recognized that the next attempt to reinforce Fort Sumter would not be by an unarmed commercial ship but by a fleet of naval ships capable of raking the island with powerful broadsides. He drew up a plan to add detached batteries, two heavy guns in each, well protected by sand traverses from fire from the sides and separated from each other by fifty to one hundred yards to minimize the impact of broadsides from warships. This amounted to a total of twenty guns in all along the shipping channel. Having seen the fortress from all sides, he wrote the Confederate secretary of war, Leroy Pope Walker, "Fort Sumter, properly garrisoned and armed would be a perfect Gibraltar to anything but constant bombardment around the clock from the four points of the compass." Morris Island was to have a big part in doing just that a month and a half later.

Construction of Beauregard's shore batteries was assigned to his chief engineer on Morris Island, Major William Henry Chase Whiting. Whiting, a thirty-four-year old graduate of West Point, had served for eighteen years with the U.S. Army Corps of Engineers before resigning his commission to serve in the Confederate army. Whiting brought a new urgency to Morris Island's defenses, and Fort Sumter's garrison witnessed what some described as one of the South's greatest strengths in action. Hundreds of African American slaves were transported to Morris Island and employed in the manual work of building and arming the gun batteries. The swell of patriotic pride induced local plantation owners to offer up their slaves for this work. Some of Charleston's small free black population saw value in volunteering to help defend the state they called home. Many free blacks would serve the city in volunteer fire companies, much needed as the white population was swept into the war machine. Beauregard also made changes to the armament of the Cummings Point batteries. He had three heavy ten-inch mortars moved from the more exposed Cummings Point Battery to the Trapier Battery, where they would be better protected from Sumter's guns.[17] The speed with which the improvements on Morris Island were completed was remarkable. Captain Francis Lee reported to Beauregard that in a little over two weeks, he had mounted seven heavy seacoast guns and two additional twenty-four pounders commanding the main shipping channel. Beauregard gave careful attention to assigning details to each of the pieces and, on March 30, ordered a massive display of the readiness of the Morris Island batteries. Beginning about 11:00 a.m. with three dips of the new South Carolina state flag from artillery headquarters, the Cummings Point Battery and the others fired off a proscribed sequence at ten-second intervals. Obviously pleased with the demonstration, on April 1, he wrote Secretary of War Pope that his batteries would be ready in four days.[18] Colonel Wilmot G. DeSaussure, his artillery commander on Morris Island, gave Beauregard a detailed account of the powder cartridges and shot and shell available for each gun in the fourteen batteries stretching from one end of the island to the other. The nearly deserted Morris Island, in the course of three months, had been converted into an armed camp with a force of over two thousand infantry and artillerymen.

In a series of communiqués with their superiors, Robert Anderson and John Foster had tried to discern the location, number and size of guns mounted on Morris Island. The display on the thirtieth gave them much more information, and a detailed account was sent by mail to Foster's superior, General Joseph G. Totten, in Washington along with an enclosed map.[19]

There was only one more piece of the puzzle, and it arrived in Charleston from Liverpool on April 7. Charles K. Prioleau, a Charlestonian serving in England as manager of the Fraser Trenholm Company, procured a twelve-pounder rifled cannon newly designed by British captain Theophilus Alexander Blakely and a limited amount of the 3.75-inch projectiles it fired with accuracy unheard of with smoothbore cannons; he gifted this innovation in cannon design to the state. This small Blakely would have been a mere footnote to the tons of heavy weaponry arrayed on the island, but the rifle's performance during the bombardment of Fort Sumter launched an arms race that would reach its zenith at Morris Island two years later. The "Rifle," as the Confederates called it, was placed in the Cummings Point Battery, from which it fired thirty rounds at Fort Sumter.

All of the optimism about a peaceful solution to the problem of Fort Sumter and rumors of planned evacuations of the garrison evaporated on April 8, when Robert S. Chew of the U.S. State Department met first with Governor Pickens separately and then with the governor and General Beauregard to inform them that President Lincoln intended to resupply Fort Sumter with force if necessary. Gustavus Fox, who had been allowed to confer with Anderson on the evening of March 21 at Fort Sumter and was Lincoln's handpicked leader of the expedition, is likely to have informed Anderson of his plan, which involved sending in men and materiel at night on small boats that could cross the bar at any point. On orders from the capital at Montgomery, Beauregard stopped all mail to and from Fort Sumter on April 8. Anderson, now isolated from Washington and cut off

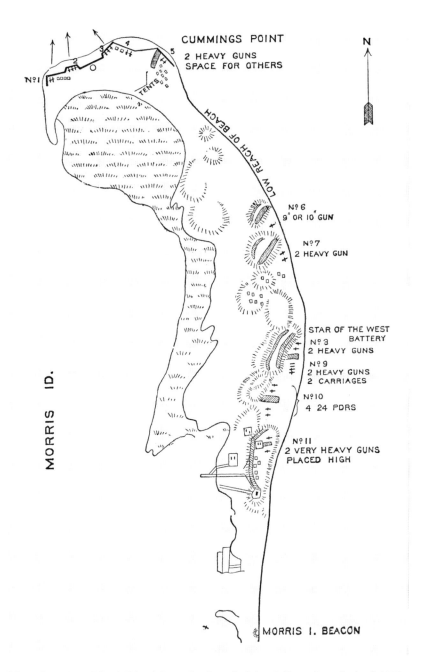

Map of northern Morris Island drawn by Captain John G. Foster in early April 1861. *From* The War of the Rebellion: A Compilation of the Official Records of the Union and Confederate Armies, *Series 1, Vol. 1 (Washington, D.C.: Government Printing Office, 1880), 244.*

from food and communication, would be left to determine the fate of his garrison and of the nation. Beauregard was informed of the approach of Fox's expedition on April 11, when the U.S. revenue cutter *Harriet Lane* arrived off Charleston, and sent aides to Fort Sumter to demand Anderson's evacuation of the fort.[20] When he indicated he would not comply, Colonel James Chesnut, Colonel James A. Chisholm and Captain Steven D. Lee, after conferring for two hours, informed Major Anderson at 3:20 a.m. on April 12 that General Beauregard would open fire from his batteries in one hour. The aides were immediately conveyed by skiff to Fort Johnson on James Island to communicate orders to commence firing at the appointed time and reached the post at 4:00 a.m. While it is commonly thought that a single shot marked the opening of the bombardment, there were actually three nearly simultaneous shots from two different mortar batteries at 4:30 a.m. Only one exploded over the fort, and it is not possible to say from which battery that shot came. Two officers—Lieutenants Henry S. Farley and Wade Hampton Gibbes, both with credible witnesses—would go to their graves believing they had fired the first shot of the Civil War. Farley was at a mortar in the Beach Battery and Gibbes was a few hundred yards away at the Hill Battery, both of which were outside of Fort Johnson proper. Accounts vary, but most report that almost simultaneous to the firing of the mortars, a deafening roar marked the demolition of a house in front of the Hill Battery, which no doubt contributed to the confusion.[21] In attempting to analyze how something as historically significant at the first shot of the Civil War could be shrouded in controversy, one must first consider the reliability of the weapons involved. There are five points at which a signal shot could fail. The first is the friction primer, which sent a jet of flame through the vent of the cannon into the powder charge. The second is the propelling charge itself, which could fail to ignite. The third is the igniting of the powder-filled shell's delay fuse on the discharge of the propelling charge. Fourth is the timed burning of the fuse. Finally, the fine-grained bursting powder must explode on ignition by the fuse. Mortars, because of their high-arcing trajectory, require long delay fuses. During the Civil War, mortar fuses were typically hollow, powder-filled conical wooden plugs that were driven into the shell. The powder was compacted and the burn rate experimentally determined for each batch of fuses. To aid in ignition, the top of the powder tube was enlarged and primed with dust-like mealed powder that was moistened with flammable alcohol to aide in ignition. The fuse would be cut to length based on the indicated burn rate and the range table for the mortar. About a half-inch of the plug protruded from the shell so that it could be removed for adjustment. The burning of the fuse emitted sparks, which could be seen at night as the shell flew to its target. Given all the possibilities for failure, a prudent officer would have employed two mortars to signal the batteries to open fire.[22] Farley's accounts were defended by a physician, Dr. Robert Lebby, while others said that it was common knowledge in Charleston at the start of the war that Lieutenant Gibbes was ordered by Captain George S. James to fire the signal shot.[23] Gibbes's account further cites that his battery fired two shots: the first was designed as a signal burst, while the second was aimed to fall into the fort.[24] Thus we have not one but up to three shots fired. Many of the Fort Sumter garrison, unable to sleep, waited on its parapets throughout the night and saw the mortars roar and, almost thirty seconds later, the shell burst overhead. Lieutenant Richard Meade, who resigned his commission to join the Confederacy, told Gibbes that he had seen his solid shot fall into the parade.

The first batteries to open on Fort Sumter after the mortar burst were at Fort Moultrie, responding about fifteen minutes after the signal. Morris Island's Trapier Battery mortars responded next, followed by the Cummings

View from Fort Moultrie during the opening bombardment. Cummings Point batteries are on the extreme left and the floating battery on the extreme right. *From Ben La Bree et al.,* Pictorial Battles of the Civil War *(New York: Sherman Publishing, 1885).*

Point Battery. As it was not yet daylight, the Stevens Ironclad Battery waited until dawn to be able to aim its Columbiads at the fort. So it was almost an hour after the bombardment opened that the venerable Edmund Ruffin was given the honor of firing the first shot from the ironclad battery. Historians would incorrectly memorialize his role in the start of the Civil War.

While the details of the around-the-clock bombardment that lasted about thirty hours have been reported elsewhere, it is important for the reader appreciate that Morris Island played a major part in the shelling that led to Major Anderson agreeing to evacuate the burning fort. Of the slightly over 3,000 shots and shells fired at Fort Sumter from the surrounding batteries, Morris Island's batteries contributed 976 of them.[25]

Anderson, undermanned and practically out of supplies, fought the good fight and somehow managed to bring his small garrison and loyal workmen through the battle without loss of life or limb. Beauregard treated his former West Point artillery instructor with dignity, allowing him, his soldiers and loyal workmen to salute his flag and leave the fort with flags and weapons on Sunday, April 14.[26] Perhaps Beauregard should have been a little less liberal in his concessions, because in his generosity, things went terribly wrong for the major. Not content with a normal salute to the flag, Anderson ordered a one-hundred-gun salute. Two batteries of five guns each were assigned to participate, necessitating ten cartridges per gun. On the left flank parapet, an arrangement of metal plates for the intended second-tier Totten shutters had been placed against the interior of the five-foot wall that surrounded the top of the fort. The reserve cartridges were placed behind this lean-to affair. At about the forty-seventh or forty-eighth salute, the reserve cartridges for one of the guns exploded, hurling one of the iron plates into gunner Private Daniel Hough, a native of county Cork, Ireland, killing him instantly. The force blew another member of the crew, Private Edward Gallway, also of Cork, off of the parapet.[27] The forty-foot fall broke many bones and left Gallway mortally wounded. A third member of the crew was badly burned. The accident caused the salute to be stopped at fifty rounds. Private Hough was buried in the fort's parade with full military honors by the garrison. The Charleston doctor who had been called to attend the wounded had them transported to a hospital in Charleston, where Gallway died shortly after arriving.[28] The burned soldier recovered and was given passage north. The burial and preparations complete, Anderson and his garrison marched out of the fort and boarded the small sidewheel steamer *General Clinch*, tied up to the Fort Sumter dock. The *General Clinch* then transported the garrison to the oceangoing sidewheel steamer *Isabel*, anchored nearby.[29] The accident and burial delayed the departure, and the high tide had been missed, preventing the deep-draft steamer from crossing the bar. The weary garrison was forced to spend the night in earshot of the fort they had tried but failed to hold. In the morning, they crossed the bar and were transferred to the steamer *Baltic* for passage to New York. They and the Fort Sumter flags were welcomed in New York by huge crowds, crowning the garrison with glory and screaming for revenge.

However convoluted, these events—large and small—played a part in establishing Fort Sumter as the place where the Civil War began. For generations, every student in America has learned this, and over half a million visitors come each year to view the ruins preserved by the National Park Service. Few appreciate the role that the peaceful-looking island nearest to the fort played not only in starting the war but also in changing the very nature of warfare.

Chapter 2

MORRIS ISLAND DEFENSES ABANDONED

The Fall of Fort Pulaski, General John C. Pemberton and His Troubled Command

F ort Sumter, now in the hands of the Confederate States of America, was quickly restored to full fighting trim. The brick remnants of the badly burned quarters were taken down, debris cleared away and new quarters prepared in the rooms under the gorge wall arches and in unused second-tier casemates. Dismounted cannons were repaired, and the large openings in the second tier were closed with brick, leaving only loopholes for rifles. Colonel Roswell Ripley of the South Carolina First Artillery was in charge of this work and reported to General Beauregard that the fort would be ready for action by the end of April. Beauregard would have his perfect Gibraltar, armed and manned to defend Charleston from the sea. He then saw Morris Island in a different light. All of the works that had been built on the island to bombard Fort Sumter were not only useless now that he held the fort, they were a potential threat should Union forces occupy Morris Island. It was feared that the navy would try to force a landing from the main shipping channel in a flat spot between Lighthouse Hill and Vinegar Hill. Beauregard ordered all of the guns, with the exception of two light fieldpieces, moved to Vinegar Hill in the middle of the island and to Oyster Point on the southern end. Once the guns were removed, he wanted all the gun positions, protective traverses and parapets leveled so they would be of no use to the enemy.[30] His chief engineer, Major William Henry Whiting, wrote Beauregard in confidence suggesting all of the defenses could be removed from Morris Island because Fort Sumter and Fort Moultrie were more than adequate to defend the harbor. Beauregard bought into Whiting's

Map used by General Gillmore covers the area of operation against Morris Island and includes Folly Island and James Island. *Courtesy of the Library of Congress.*

logic and wrote the secretary of war telling him that he planned to withdraw all guns and troops from Morris Island.[31]

Helping General Beauregard prepare a rifle battery at Vinegar Hill was Ambrose Jose Gonzales, a Cuban exile with deep ties to the leaders of the Confederacy. Beauregard informed Gonzales that he was abandoning the idea of more batteries for Morris Island and wanted him to transfer the guns to Fort Pickens on Battery Island and Fort Palmetto on Cole's Island to reinforce the Stono River defenses.[32]

Ambrose Jose Gonzales was a leader in the aborted Cuban independence movement and had sought refuge in the United States after being sentenced to death. He married into the wealthy Lowcountry family of William Elliott and was well known in Washington circles. He lobbied for annexation of the island nation with Southern politicos, including Jefferson Davis. On learning of the firing on Fort Sumter, he strapped on his sword, took the train from the Elliott family winter home at Oak Lawn Plantation about thirty miles south of Charleston and offered his assistance to General Beauregard. They were known to each other before the war began.[33] Gonzales, believing himself fit for higher command, frequently petitioned Jefferson Davis for a generalship, reminding Davis of the assistance Gonzales had rendered in Davis's senatorial races. By October 16, 1861, the pandering became more than Davis could stand, and he wrote a stern letter of rebuke, essentially ending their friendship.[34] Fortunately, Gonzales's connections earned him a position as chief of artillery, Department of South Carolina, Georgia and Florida, in June 1862.[35] He served in that capacity for the remainder of the war and made many important contributions to the defense of Charleston.

While a restored Fort Sumter emboldened Beauregard to abandon Morris Island, there were ports in Georgetown, north of Charleston, and Port Royal, to the south, with no defenses at all. The Edisto River was also a point of vulnerability. He undertook a personal inspection of the coastal defense needs, and on May 15, he communicated his findings to Governor Pickens with regard to points south of Charleston. He recognized that the Port Royal entrance would require special attention and recommended that a floating battery, such as he used at Charleston, be moored in mid-channel between forts to be built on either side of the entrance.[36] Before he could finish his plans for Georgetown, he was needed elsewhere.

Lincoln's April 15, 1861 proclamation for seventy-five thousand troops to invade the South in response to the firing on Fort Sumter and telegrams to the governors from Simon Cameron, secretary of war, with requisitions for regiments produced two distinctly different reactions. Some states were overjoyed, offering as many regiments as would be needed, and others replied instantly that the call was unconstitutional. It is not clear whether Lincoln appreciated that the call to arms would cause even more Southern states to secede, but Virginia, Arkansas, Tennessee and North Carolina followed the original seven. His call had forced them into declaring allegiance to their Southern neighbors. Lincoln now had an even bigger problem than Fort Sumter. Northern states had just the opposite reaction. They were all in to avenge Fort Sumter and immediately began mobilizing and training regiments to invade the South.

It is hard to say which side was less prepared to go to war. One might think the Union had deep resources to draw on, but on the eve of the war, the U.S. Army consisted of fewer that seventeen thousand officers and men spread from coast to coast, some in posts in the West from which they could not be withdrawn, and many whose true allegiances were with their states were resigning. The U.S. Navy was not without its share of resignations among its nine thousand officers and men and counted fewer than one hundred ships of all classes in service.[37] The capture of arsenals and shipyards in the

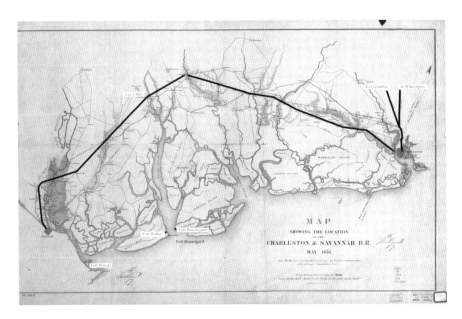

The railroad network connecting Savannah, Charleston and Wilmington was vital to the Confederate defense of the cities. *From* The War of the Rebellion: A Compilation of the Official Records of the Union and Confederate Armies, *Series 1, Vol. 28, Part 2 (Washington, D.C.: Government Printing Office, 1890), 115. Locations of forts and branches to Columbia and Wilmington identified by author.*

seceded states was a significant loss of weapons and machinery. The South had the advantage of the interior lines, and individual states had made investments in weapons prior to the conflict and could draw on well-trained militia units. The organizational structure of the Union's armed forces was clearly a head start, though the policy of not retiring aging officers made it less than perfect. The South had a blank slate and began with the long view of establishing a limited permanent army with career officers and enlisted men. The South's response to Lincoln's seventy-five-thousand-man call up to invade the seceded states would be met by the Provisional Confederate States Army (PCSA), largely composed of state militia units that were merged into it. To make the structure even more complicated, the fiercely independent states maintained their own home guards and engineering and supply departments.

With Virginia throwing its lot with the South, the immediate reaction of the government was to concentrate what men were available into the Washington, D.C. area to protect the nation's capital. Toward the end of May, it was decided that Richmond, the center of manufacturing in the

South and with much better infrastructure, would be a better capital city than Montgomery. The Confederate capital was now less than one hundred miles from Washington, making it a likely target for the anticipated reaction to the affront at Fort Sumter. With all eyes focused on Northern Virginia, Beauregard was ordered to Virginia and given command of what would become the Army of the Potomac. He left the defensive works in South Carolina in the hands of Colonel Richard H. Anderson. Anderson was a native son of South Carolina and a West Point graduate serving in the regular army. To quell some of the uneasiness of the change of command, he informed Governor Pickens of some of his plans for defense. In particular, he told of installing a telegraph line across the new bridge over the Ashley River and opening telegraphic communication between the city and the harbor forts and the Stono River batteries.

The three officers left in Charleston were all given commissions in the PCSA despite their markedly different backgrounds. Colonel Ripley was left in charge of the Charleston harbor forts, and Captain Thomas Wagner was in direct command of Fort Sumter. Ripley was an outsider—Ohio-born and West Point–educated—who served in the artillery in the Mexican-American War and was posted to Fort Moultrie, where he retired from the U.S. Army in 1853 after marrying into a prominent Charleston family. He served as the colonel in command at Fort Moultrie during the bombardment of Fort Sumter and was praised by General Beauregard. In late August, Ripley was promoted to brigadier general in charge of the Department of South Carolina with responsibility for all coastal defenses. The outspoken Ripley was not pleased with the length of time it took for his abilities to be recognized and let his Charleston supporters know it.

James Heyward Trapier, who had been charged with improving defenses on Morris Island, was a true South Carolinian. He was born on a rice plantation near Georgetown. A West Point graduate, he served in the Mexican-American War and retired to Georgetown at the age of thirty-three to become a planter and officer in the South Carolina militia. As chief ordnance officer for the state, he was instrumental in procuring many of the heavy guns used to reduce Fort Sumter from the Tredegar Iron Works in Richmond, Virginia. With little to do on Morris Island, which it appeared the war had passed by, Trapier was transferred to the Florida District in October 1861.[38]

Francis Dickinson Lee was tasked with protecting Port Royal, the largest deep-water port on the southeast coast. Lee was an accomplished architect who designed a number of notable structures in Charleston. He was a Charleston native and a graduate of the College of Charleston. Lee learned architecture from the firm of Edwin C. Jones.[39] Jones and Lee had designed the Institute Hall, where the ordinance of secession was signed. Lee's architectural skills were invaluable in the fortifications he designed to defend the coast of South Carolina throughout the war, but he was also an inventor of amazing talent. Among his successful inventions was the Lee torpedo: an explosive charge mounted on a spar designed to be lowered and raised by means of cables from the bow of boats that would exploded on contact with an enemy vessel. Lee's invention included a specially designed fuse that would only detonate when the explosive charge was under water. A Lee torpedo was carried by the Confederate submarine *Hunley*, which sank the USS *Housatonic* late in the war.[40] He proposed designing a fleet of small, fast boats to use against Union warships and demonstrated the capability to General Beauregard, who endorsed Lee's proposal. After the war, Lee moved his architecture practice to St. Louis.

Brigadier General Roswell S. Ripley was responsible for the incomplete fortifications at Lighthouse Inlet on Morris Island. *Courtesy of the Library of Congress.*

Charlestonian Francis D. Lee was a gifted architect and inventor. He designed Battery Wagner and other Confederate fortifications. *Courtesy of the South Carolina Historical Society.*

In 1861, Francis Lee was more concerned with how he could defend the entrance to Port Royal Sound and the wealthy rice plantations of the Beaufort area. The two-mile-wide deep-water channel was nearly impossible to defend. The smoothbore guns that were available did not have the range to command a channel of that width, and the open space and depth gave naval ships plenty of room to maneuver. Lee did the best he could designing and helping to erect formidable earthworks on Hilton Head Island to the south and at Bay Point to the north, called Fort Walker and Fort Beauregard, respectively.

While Ripley, Lee and Trapier labored along the coast, Beauregard assembled his army and prepared to counter a movement toward Richmond by General Irvin McDowell's Army of Northeastern Virginia. At the battle of Manassas, on July 21, 1861, Beauregard earned his stars as a field commander, but soon after, cracks began to develop in his relationship with Jefferson Davis that would have a major role in the fate of Morris Island. The immediate source of the disagreement was Beauregard's stinging rebuke of Davis's handpicked quartermaster for the Confederacy, Colonel Lucius Bellinger Northrup, blaming the commissary for his inability to capture Washington in the wake of his victory. Beauregard's rebuke was in a letter to his aide that was somehow read before the Confederate Congress and gave fuel to an ever-growing anti-Davis faction in the Congress. Reading *The Military Operations of General Beauregard*, one can see that the general was as much a politician as a soldier and did not confine his energies to matters military. This characteristic certainly would not have endeared him to the president.

The Union armies reorganized in the wake of the stunning defeat at Manassas, but the U.S. Navy was having a field day on the coast of North Carolina, capturing exposed forts and looking to extend its success to the south. By early November, a major expeditionary force under Admiral Samuel F. Du Pont was rumored to be heading to South Carolina or Georgia. Jefferson Davis ordered Robert E. Lee to take charge of the defenses of South Carolina, Georgia and Florida. Lee, passing through Charleston, arrived at the tiny rail stop of Coosawatchie, South Carolina, about sixty miles south of the city, on the evening of November 7, just two days after receiving orders. This was the closest rail point to Port Royal, where Du Pont was concentrating his fleet, about thirty miles to the southeast. By the time Lee arrived, there was nothing he could do. On his way to the coast by horseback, he met Roswell Ripley, who broke the news to Lee that early that day Admiral Du Pont's fleet pounded the Confederate's defenses at Port Royal with its combined firepower, forcing the garrisons to abandon the works and flee. The battle was over in four hours and convinced Lee of the vulnerability of outposts like Forts Walker and Beauregard that were exposed to naval assault. This principle would have a major impact on the fate of Morris Island. Sensing Ripley was overextended, on November 17, Lee reorganized the coastal defense and reduced Ripley's command to the Charleston defenses.

The presence of the enemy on South Carolina soil in greater numbers than all of the Confederate defenders created a great sense of alarm in the state. Toward the end of November, Jefferson Davis, responding to concerns from Governor Francis Pickens, sent one of Davis's favorites, Brigadier General John C. Pemberton, to assist Lee. Lee divided the coast of South Carolina into five districts, giving Pemberton the district surrounding Port Royal with his headquarters in Coosawatchie with Lee.

While concentrating forces to prevent the Union from moving inland from Port Royal, Lee began to appreciate how important the rail connection between Wilmington, Charleston and Savannah was to the defenses of these important ports. He traveled between the cities to inspect the defensives works and was in Charleston on December 11, staying at the Mills House on the corner of Meeting and Queen Streets, when a fire of suspicious origins broke out at low tide on a night with exceedingly high winds. Forced to abandon his lodgings, the general watched as the efforts of General Ripley to contain the fire by blowing up buildings failed. The fire burned completely across the peninsula, only ending when it ran out of fuel after consuming some six hundred structures. Rumors that the fire was an act of servile insurrection could not be confirmed. The Great Fire would leave Charleston scarred for years, with little capacity to rebuild during the war— although the war would wreak havoc, it was nothing compared to the fire. Little did the soon-to-be great general realize that there was another fire smoldering in Charleston, and he was adding fuel to it. Reducing Ripley's sphere of command by limiting him to focus on the Charleston defenses may have been a better approach to managing two hundred miles of coastline, but the order did not sit well with Ripley. Ripley's dislike for Lee would track his "contumacious" relations with all of his superiors during the war. His days of directly reporting to the general were numbered.[41]

On his return to his headquarters at Coosawatchie, Lee learned that Charleston was unlikely to be the immediate focus of the growing U.S. military presence in Port Royal. Observers at Charleston reported that a fleet of old ships was being accumulated off the bar by the U.S. Navy. The intent was clear: to sink these ships to block the harbor entrance. On the evening of December 18, General Ripley ordered the brick Charleston Lighthouse on Morris Island blown up to prevent the U.S. Navy from using the landmark to locate where to enter the ship channel from the open ocean.[42] The destruction of the lighthouse had little impact on the operation, which located the passage by sounding the bar and scuttled the sixteen stone-filled vessels across its width.[43] To Lee, this was sound evidence that with the Union holding nearby Port Royal and advancing on Tybee Island near Fort Pulaski, he should concentrate his efforts on Savannah's defenses.

What Lee did not know was that Thomas West Sherman and Quincy Gillmore were busy analyzing the prospects for capturing Charleston from their base a few miles away at Hilton Head. One year to the day after Robert Anderson made his move to Fort Sumter, they presented their plan to deal with the problem of Charleston to General George McClellan. They gave him several options that showed an amazing amount of details on the local geography and how the forts could be either reduced or bypassed.

Thomas W. Sherman was an artillerist of the old army. A West Point graduate in the class of 1836, he had commanded artillery in the Mexican-American War and was posted to Fort Ridgely, Minnesota, an artillery field school before the Civil War.[44] His first major command in the war was as brevet general of volunteers in charge of the land forces for the Port Royal expedition, where he met Captain Quincy Adams Gillmore, chief engineer for the expedition. Gillmore was top of his 1849 class at West Point and was appointed to the Corps of Engineers, as was customary for that honor. Like most of the top graduates of West Point, he became involved in construction of the third system of coastal defense. In 1856, he became a purchasing agent for the Corps of Engineers, where he filled requests for materials for Fort Sumter and other projects. With the advent of the telegraph system and regularly scheduled packet ships running between New York and Charleston, it was possible to get hardware orders from Fort Sumter's engineering office on the corner of Hasell and King Streets in Charleston to Gillmore's office in New York and on a ship the same day. Three days later, the items would be at the docks in Charleston. His work on Fort Sumter and other third-system forts gave him knowledge about their vulnerabilities. As was recognized at Fort Sumter in the opening battle, the Fortification Board that designed these forts wanted them to be self-sufficient for two weeks under siege. A single ten-inch Columbiad firing every ten minutes for eight hours could consume almost five hundred pounds of powder. This meant large amounts of powder were stored within the forts, and at Fort Sumter, this proved to be a point of vulnerability. Although Gillmore's academic record and postwar expertise in concrete were evidence of his high intelligence, there is nothing in his background that suggested that he was an expert in artillery when he started the expedition. In preparing his plan of attack on Charleston, he may have drawn on General Thomas Sherman's knowledge of artillery.

The plan recognized that bypassing the forts and attacking Charleston overland either from Bull's Bay to the north or the Stono River to the south would render them useless. He felt that capturing Morris and Sullivan's Islands and reducing Forts Sumter and Moultrie, followed by the navy entering the harbor and bombarding the city, was less desirable than attacking via James Island, because the Stone Fleet obstructing the harbor meant the navy could not cooperate, and reducing the forts did not necessarily mean the city would capitulate. He estimated that fourteen thousand infantry, one thousand cavalry, twelve light guns and twenty siege guns, including a "large proportion" of twenty- and thirty-pounder Parrott rifles, would be needed for the plan to succeed.[45]

The Parrott rifles he wanted were the invention of Captain Robert Parker Parrott, a retired army officer who in 1860 developed a unique way of reinforcing the breech of a cast-iron rifled cannon. Applying the principle of rifling that had been practiced in shoulder weapons and pistols for many years to large cannons had proved problematic. For a weapon of the same caliber, rifling required an elongated projectile, so that a three-inch smoothbore cannonball was lighter than a three-inch rifle projectile. Accelerating the rifle projectile to the same velocity therefore required a greater force. In a cannon, the peak force is realized in the breech just as the projectile starts moving, and the resulting pressure of the larger charges put too much force on the breech for the cast iron to withstand. One might think the problem could be solved by adding thickness to the breech, but it is the nature of pressure that once the yield point is exceeded cracks form. The cracks provide more surface area for the pressure to act upon, which causes the metal to yield further until it ultimately fails. Steel, which had the strength necessary, was too expensive in the quantities needed for cannons, and bronze wore too fast. The problem was solved by Captain Blakely and others by reinforcing the breech with a stronger metal. While Parrott did not claim to have invented rifling in cannons, he did invent a novel way of reinforcing the brittle cast-iron breech. Whereas the British designers like Blakely created wrought-iron bands separately then heated and forced them over the cannon's breech, Parrott's invention was to form the rings directly on the cannon by turning the cannon while wrapping a red hot wrought-iron band around it in a spiral while the bore was cooled with water. Parrott's theory was that his method prevented the band from hanging on a high spot and therefore applied a more uniform support for the breech.[46] The twenty- and thirty-pounders mentioned by Quincy Gillmore were first used in battle at Manassas, where a thirty-pounder fired the opening shot of the battle. Parrotts captured at the battle were used as models for Confederate-manufactured copies. Gillmore was probably not aware at the time that Robert Parrott was busy designing even larger rifles at the West Point Foundry, at Cold Springs across the river from the U.S. Military Academy.

Lee's tenure on the coast was not long enough for him to witness the application of rifled cannons to expose the weakness of masonry forts like Pulaski. He had been impressed with the navy's ability to mass firepower but doubted that the army could breach the thick walls of the third-system forts from nearby islands. He felt his improvements to Fort Pulaski, which he helped build, would allow the garrison to hold out even though Union artillery commanded the river, effectively cutting off a vital supply line. Gillmore methodically erected breaching batteries and prepared for a lengthy bombardment of the fort.

Before Lee could be recalled to Richmond, a change in the command structure for his department was needed. There is little evidence that John Pemberton did anything in his area of command carved out by Lee to deserve promotion, but having friends in high places can do wonders for one's career. A West Point graduate, Pemberton was a native of Pennsylvania who, like Ripley, had become a Southerner by marriage. Described as a martinet who projected better to his superiors than to his subordinates, he was destined to be promoted beyond his level of competency.[47] He was nominated for promotion to major general on January 10 and confirmed on January 14. A month later, Pemberton learned of his promotion and moved his headquarters to Pocotaligo. On March 3, 1862, only a month after moving his headquarters to Savannah, Lee was recalled to Richmond. Pemberton then temporarily assumed command of the Department of South Carolina. On March 14, the secretary of war permanently assigned Pemberton to command of both South Carolina and Georgia but separated Florida under General Trapier. On April 7, he extended Pemberton's command to include most of Florida and placed General States Rights Gist under Pemberton in command of South Carolina. The next six months were full of events that would have derailed the career of the average major general, but Pemberton would just shake them off and move ever closer to his surrender at Vicksburg.

Pemberton's problems began at 8:15 a.m. on April 10. U.S. major general David Hunter had relieved Brigadier General Thomas Sherman on March 31 and assumed command of the Department of the South, which included Union operations in South Carolina, Georgia and Florida.[48] He sent a dawn demand to Confederate colonel Charles Olmstead, commander of Fort Pulaski, to surrender. When this was refused, the Union opened its batteries against Fort Pulaski. Lee's confidence in the fort's strength proved unfounded in the face of Parrott and James rifles. James rifles were smoothbore cannons that had been rifled by broaching spiraling grooves in the bore, an invention of Charles T. James. As the inner diameter of the cannon remained the same, by elongating the projectile, they roughly doubled the weight. Hence a thirty-two-pound smoothbore firing round balls became a sixty-four-pound James rifle, and a forty-two-pound smoothbore modified by the James pattern became an eighty-four pounder. On April 11, the vaunted Fort Pulaski fell after its five-foot-thick brick walls were breached, exposing its principal powder magazine to direct fire.

The mastermind behind the operation against Fort Pulaski was forty-year-old Brigadier General Quincy Adams Gillmore. Gillmore had been brought to the attention of the president several months earlier, when William Denison, the governor of Ohio, recommended that he be promoted from captain of engineers to brigadier general. The president declined, but Sherman, recognizing that Gillmore would need greater authority to command the siege operation, pushed the issue with General George McClellan, while Gillmore himself lobbied chief engineer Joseph Totten. Sherman went out on a limb and promoted Gillmore to acting brigadier general of the U.S. Volunteers on January 22, 1861, subject to the approval of the president. The promotion did not sit well with others in Hunter's command who were senior in service to Gillmore, especially artillery captain John Hamilton.[49] With great difficulty, Gillmore managed to erect the siege batteries from February 21 to April 9. He directed the transfer of the heavy cannons from ships to small boats and had them rowed ashore at high tide to be dumped in the surf. From their position on the beach, he would employ as many as 250 men to haul the thirty-six cannons over the marsh bog to the eleven batteries. Considering the difficulties he encountered, it was an amazing feat to accomplish in just six weeks, much of it at night to avoid fire from Fort Pulaski. From this and previous batteries he constructed on marsh islands on the Savannah River, he learned much about conditions on the barrier islands, including the "soft unctuous mud" that surrounds the high ground on marsh islands and the value of rifled artillery against masonry forts.[50] He also learned much about self-promotion, attributing success of the operation to himself, much to the dismay of Generals David Hunter and Henry W. Benham, who had given him the tools he needed to accomplish the mission.[51] The final lesson learned was that working in the subtropical swamps was hazardous to one's health—he acquired malaria in the mosquito-infested area. After a period of sick leave and assisting the governor of New York with recruits, he, like Beauregard, found himself transferred to the West, principally in Kentucky.[52]

The fall of Fort Pulaski after such a brief bombardment was no doubt a great shock to the engineers like Robert E. Lee who labored for so many years to construct the masonry forts guarding America's harbors. Its impact on the situation at Fort Sumter was huge and convoluted. Before Lee left the command, he had written Charleston's commander, Roswell Ripley, practically ordering him to abandon the defenses that had been constructed on Cole's Island to prevent ships from entering the Stono River. In his view, these were exactly the kind of batteries that were vulnerable to naval attack and would fall as quickly as Port Royal. Lee impressed his views upon his successor, and Pemberton, in turn, shared this opinion with irascible Ripley. General Pemberton was determined to follow Lee's advice and evacuate exposed positions, and he was loathe to build new ones on barrier islands.[53] But after Fort Pulaski fell, General Ripley knew Fort Sumter would suffer the same fate if the Union placed artillery on Morris Island and insisted that General Pemberton fortify the island. Pemberton reluctantly surveyed the island by horseback in April 1862 and determined that the ideal defensive position against a land advance was a point near the lazaretto approximately three-quarters of a mile south of Cummings Point.[54] The existing boat landing and easy access to Charleston Harbor via Vincent's Creek also made this point ideal from a logistical perspective. Strategically, the site made use of the island's geography, because immediately south of this point was a narrow waist in the island where the salt marsh came within 75 yards of meeting the ocean. Despite its obvious defensive advantages, the location was only 2,700 yards from Fort Sumter, much too close to protect the fort from improved land-based artillery fire. Whether this deficiency was immediately apparent is not known, but one only had to examine the ranges of the siege batteries at Fort Pulaski and the capability of Parrott rifles to realize that allowing artillery to be placed within 3,400 yards of Fort Sumter could spell trouble. Ripley felt that the position chosen by Pemberton was not ideal for the only fortification on the island, because it could not be supported by Forts Moultrie and Johnson as effectively as a position at Cummings Point. Ripley was unsuccessful in convincing Pemberton about the new battery and was equally as ineffective in changing Pemberton's mind about abandoning the Cole's Island batteries.

Pemberton was not ignorant of the threat posed by not defending the Stono River access to Charleston and ordered two additional batteries on James Island that were not as exposed as Ripley's batteries on the marsh island. These included a large earthwork far up the Stono, where a bend gave the fort an excellent command of the river. This large twenty-gun earthwork became known as Fort Pemberton. The second work he began was designed to protect an observation tower the Confederates built on a peninsula known to locals as Secessionville. The tall tower allowed the defenders to observe the Stono River entrance. Charlestonian Colonel Lewis M. Hatch possessed an intimate knowledge of the rivers, creeks, marshes and islands of the Carolina Lowcountry, and he determined exactly where the Tower Battery should be located to take maximum advantage of the topography.[55] Neither of these works could prevent entrance into the Stono or landing on James Island. Ripley, meanwhile, had begun building another battery on a shallow spot in Charleston Harbor between Castle Pinckney and Fort Johnson called the Middle Ground. This battery, which would eventually be named Battery Ripley after its creator, was constructed by creating a log cribwork and filling it with tons of bricks available in the burned district of the city. It was designed to mount four guns.[56]

Design and construction of the defenses ordered by Pemberton fell on the engineering department at Charleston and, in particular, upon architect Francis D. Lee, noted for his remodeling of Charleston's Unitarian Church and the Farmers and Exchange Bank with partner Edward C. Jones.[57] Captain Lee's experience at Fort Walker no doubt colored his design for Battery Wagner. He had not only designed Fort Walker, he also supervised its construction and then participated in the battle with Admiral Du Pont's fleet.[58]

Civilians also either volunteered or were employed by the engineering department.[59] One such civilian who became intimately involved in building the new work on Morris Island was Langdon Cheves Jr., a forty-eight-year-old planter from Jasper County near Savannah. He had inherited his Savannah River plantation from his father and owned 264 slaves at the beginning of the Civil War.[60] Langdon was experienced in managing groups of slaves in repairing rice field dikes but had no training in military engineering. At the beginning of the war, he became involved with building earthworks to defend landings along the Savannah River.

Ripley was adamantly opposed to General Lee's concept of abandoning the batteries guarding the entrance to the Stono. When Pemberton ordered Ripley to remove the guns he had at Cole's and Battery Islands, this fact was soon to be known to the Federal forces by a remarkable coincidence. The vessel Ripley used to remove the guns was a shallow-draft sidewheel steamer known as the *Planter*, operating under charter to the Confederate government with an eleven-man crew composed of eight enslaved African Americans under a white captain, mate and engineer. One of the crew members was Robert Smalls, whose knowledge of the waters and the ship led him to function as the pilot of the vessel. Robert had been born into slavery in the Mckee family of Beaufort, where his enslaved mother was a cook. When Robert was in his early teens, he was sent to Charleston to be hired out first as a streetlamp lighter and later as a stevedore and a crew member of the *Planter*. Robert was well aware of the presence of the Union blockade ships outside of Charleston Harbor and began plotting with his fellow crewmen to escape slavery to the safety of those ships.

It was the habit of the captain and mate to go ashore when the *Planter* was in port. Robert saw this as an opportunity to commandeer the vessel and determined that May 12, 1862, would be the day to do it. It so happened that the day before, the *Planter* had removed the controversial cannons from the Stono defenses and docked at Ripley's headquarters on the Southern Wharf, adjacent to the Charleston Battery. They were to distribute the cannons to the Middle Ground Battery (Battery Ripley) under construction in Charleston Harbor the next day.[61] Robert planned to take his wife, Lydia, and children to freedom, but it was too dangerous for them to come to the Southern Wharf, which was guarded by sentries who were on alert because just two weeks earlier, on the night of April 27, Allen Davis and fourteen other slaves who worked for Ripley and had detailed knowledge of Ripley's plans managed to escape the harbor by commandeering the general's barge from the same location and rowing five hours to the USS *Bienville* on blockade duty.[62] Robert instructed his wife to take the children about a half-mile north to the Northern Wharf and wait in hiding for the *Planter*. With the captain and mate ashore, Robert made his move in the early hours of the morning. He and six crew members fired up the boilers and left for the Northern Wharf, where they picked up Lydia, Robert's children, three women, a child and another enslaved man and headed the vessel out of the harbor.[63] About daybreak, they safely passed Fort Sumter, Robert giving the appropriate signals for passage under the fort's guns. As they headed for the blockading ships, they faced their next significant danger. The blockaders were prepared to open fire on any suspicious vessel coming out of Charleston Harbor. Quick thinking produced a white sheet that Lydia had packed the family's possessions in for her dangerous trek to the Northern Wharf from their home on Union Street (now State Street). After realizing they had been given a valuable prize vessel loaded with cannons, the navy spirited the *Planter* to Port Royal and an interview with Admiral Du Pont. Smalls gave Du Pont valuable information about the disposition of forces at Charleston and, in particular, about the Stono River fortifications.

When news spread in Charleston about the loss of the valuable ship from under Ripley's eyes just two weeks after the general's barge had suffered a similar fate, things did not look good for the general. The continual arguments between Ripley and Pemberton were affecting the entire department. Finally, Ripley requested to be transferred out of the department. His wishes were soon granted, and he found yet another commander to argue with—General Daniel Harvey Hill. Ripley was with Hill until the Battle of Antietam, when a throat wound and friction with Hill had him back in Charleston to recuperate by early October 1862.[64]

The information that Robert Smalls gave to the Federals was quickly acted upon, and within two weeks, Du Pont had sent gunboats into the Stono to reconnoiter the defenses.[65] They reported that Smalls was correct; the back door to Charleston was open. David Hunter prepared an approach with two arms; one would land via the Edisto River to the south and progress overland to the Stono, where the navy would transport it to James Island. The second arm would go ashore on the abandoned landings on James Island and secure a base of operations. The navy would use its gunboats to suppress any opposition to the landings.

Operations in the winter months were usually suspended because of the difficulty of moving armies on bad roads. Charleston's weather that summer had turned into a monsoonal pattern, and roads in the area where a virtual quagmire. By the time General Horatio Wright had moved his troops across Johns Island in the incessant rain, they were exhausted, and they rested at Legareville on the south bank of the Stono. The direct arm began its landings on June 2 at Thomas Grimball's plantation and set up a perimeter around the landing. On June 8, Hunter began moving Wright's division from Legareville.[66] By June 10, Hunter had thirteen thousand troops encamped just five miles from Charleston. Alarm bells spread through the city, but the slowness of the concentration allowed time to bring in reinforcements and prepare defensive lines. General Hunter, in an extra portion of caution, determined to return to Hilton Head for additional resources and left specific instructions to his second in command, General Henry Washington Benham, not to attempt an advance toward Charleston. He added that Benham could protect his camps if threatened but was not specific as to what he considered a threat. Preparations were advanced at the Tower Battery, which was about a mile from the Federal camps, and two old twenty-four pounders that had been converted to rifles began dropping occasional shells into the Union lines and camps. With Hunter back in Hilton Head, Benham determined that the sporadic fire constituted a threat to his camps and that he would mount an assault on the Tower Battery.

Disagreeing with superior officers was not just a Confederate trait in the Civil War. Benham's plans were expressly objected to by his field commanders, Generals Isaac Stevens and Horatio Wright. To approach the Tower Battery required an advance across open fields confined on both sides by impenetrable marshes. The only way to gain an element of surprise was to maneuver troops into position under cover of darkness. Such operations are seldom accomplished as planned. Benham's plans went awry shortly after beginning, when one regiment made a wrong turn and ended up one the wrong side of a marsh from the Tower Battery. The advancing troops encountered outlying sentries; these alerted the battery, whose men were sleeping at their guns. The element of surprise gone, the first waves of troops ran into the full force of the cannons and took great casualties, becoming pinned down before the battery. Two additional waves were sent in sequentially, each in turn becoming stalled on the battlefield. The losses were severe, and when Hunter found out, he withdrew the entire expedition and put Benham up on charges that he had disobeyed orders. Immediately relieved by General Hunter, it took several months before Benham could restore his rank and reputation by proving that he was not advancing against Charleston but operating within orders to protect his camps from the guns of Battery Lamar.[67] President Lincoln revoked Benham's commission on August 7, 1862, but Benham's political connections, including four governors, swayed Lincoln to reinstate him as a lieutenant colonel of engineers five months later.[68]

The Battle of Secessionville was pivotal in the future of Union attempts to capture Charleston. As Benham argued in his defense, it was not a move against Charleston. The Tower Battery was a dead end in that regard and would only secure his camps against the Secessionville peninsula. Had he waited for Hunter to return and a concerted effort to control the heart of James Island been made with a better understanding of the topography and with his two-to-one advantage in troop strength, Charleston might have fallen without ever engaging the harbor defenses. This ill-planned four-hour battle, the largest fought on land in South Carolina in the Civil War, would shape the next three years of Charleston's Civil War history.[69]

Despite the Confederate success at Secessionville, confidence in Pemberton continued to erode in the coming months. South Carolina governor Pickens pleaded with Richmond to send him a general who would fight. A series of duels among the officers in Charleston in August and September that resulted in the death of Colonel Ransom Calhoun, Fort Sumter's commander, contributed to the decision to remove Pemberton from Charleston.[70]

Chapter 3

COMMANDERS IN CHIEF

Lincoln and Davis, the Emancipation Proclamation, the Fifty-Fourth Massachusetts and Beauregard's Troubles with Davis

I n the summer of 1862, the two warring presidents interjected themselves in strategic issues that would profoundly impact coming events at Morris Island in ways that shaped the balance of the war. Jefferson Davis, by virtue of his West Point education and service in the Mexican-American War, should have been the better commander in chief during the Civil War, but arguably Lincoln proved to be the better strategist.[71]

Lincoln's Southern counterpart was busy playing chess with his military leadership. Of particular import was his growing enmity for General Beauregard. A plan was afoot to ask the hero of Fort Sumter and Manassas to leave his Virginia army and join the efforts to defend the Mississippi Valley under Albert Sidney Johnston. The plan was presented to him toward the end of January 1862. He was informed that Congress and Davis wanted him to accept the transfer. Beauregard at first declined, citing a need to recover from a recent throat operation, but yielded to the confidence placed in him by Congress. His intuition about the situation in the West proved correct. There was nowhere near the 75,000 troops he was told were defending the vast Mississippi Valley; the true number was closer to 45,000. The Union had assembled a force of 130,000 at St. Louis and was preparing to press southward. He arrived in Bowling Green, Kentucky, on February 4 and was immediately confined to bed by his throat condition. Albert Sidney Johnston had spread his forces out, and Beauregard saw the impending disaster. Beauregard believed concentration to be the soul of war.[72] He urged Johnston to concentrate his forces and attack weak points in the Federal army. When Johnston determined to stick with his strategy, Beauregard asked to be allowed to return to Virginia. Johnston persuaded Beauregard to stay, feeling the very presence of the famous general gave confidence to the nervous populace. Beauregard's intuition was correct, as river fort after river fort fell to overwhelming Union forces, pushing the Confederate forces back south into the important rail junction of Corinth, Mississippi. There, Beauregard attempted to concentrate troops for an attack. Learning that the Union forces were at Pittsburg Landing, on the Tennessee River about twenty miles northeast of Corinth, Beauregard convinced General Johnston to make a surprise attack before they could build strength. Weather and other factors combined to make the advance from Corinth very slow, and believing the opportunity for surprise gone, the ailing Beauregard advised against attacking, but Johnston was determined. The next day, April 6, almost a year after Beauregard's success at Fort Sumter, the Battle of Shiloh began. Late in the day, General Johnston died from blood loss due to a bullet wound in his leg, and Beauregard assumed command. He ordered his troops to halt their advance at dark and lost the opportunity to win the battle. Grant reinforced his forces overnight with troops brought in by the river. The battle the next day was a Union victory, and Beauregard wisely withdrew to Corinth. The Civil War had begun to show its true horror.

Mississippi native Jefferson Davis, without knowledge of the situation, ordered Beauregard not to withdraw from Corinth. In defiance of the president's orders, Beauregard managed to withdraw all of his men and materiel to Tupelo, Mississippi, without the knowledge of the enemy. His health issues had reached a point that he could hardly function, and on the advice of his surgeons and free from immediate threat, he determined to take leave. Unfortunately, he turned his army over to the temporary command of General Braxton Bragg, knowing that Davis had other plans for Bragg. An infuriated Davis made the change permanent on June 20, 1862, by firing Beauregard, who at that time was in Mobile, Alabama, having left Tupelo on June 17. Beauregard journeyed to Bladon Springs, Alabama, about eighty miles north of Mobile, to recuperate at the mineral springs spa.[73] When Beauregard's admirers learned of this, they appealed to Davis to replace Bragg with Beauregard. He replied that he would not do so if the whole world should unite in petition. Governor Pickens of South Carolina, at wit's end over Pemberton, had written Beauregard on June 12 imploring him to return to Charleston. Beauregard replied that his health was still bad and that he was absolutely needed in Mississippi. He had plenty of time to improve his health in Alabama as the war passed him by. On August

29, Special Order 202 was sent to Beauregard and Pemberton announcing Beauregard's assignment to the Department of South Carolina and Georgia. Pemberton replied to the secretary of war that it would be humiliating in the extreme to be placed in a subordinate position and asked to be transferred.[74]

At issue for Lincoln in the second year of the war was how he could deal with the volatile issue of slavery. To believe that he was of one mind and resolved to a particular course on this issue is inconsistent with his expressed views over the course of the war. He said to Horace Greeley, the editor of the *New York Tribune*, that his goal was to preserve the Union, and he would do whatever he could to further that end. In essence, if he needed to change his views, he would.[75] Early on, he was willing to wash his hands of the issue by deferring to the Corwin Amendment and even revoked emancipation orders of Generals Benjamin Butler and David Hunter. As late as August 1862, Lincoln told Edward Salomon, the governor of Wisconsin, that he would not accept "negroes as troops."[76] When Lincoln saw the power of a different position in determining the outcome of the war, he wisely chose a new course. His decision to blockade the Southern ports caused an economic crisis in shutting off slave-produced cotton to the textile industries in New England and abroad. It is difficult today to appreciate how dependent the U.S. and foreign economies were on slavery. For the South, the capital invested in ownership of enslaved humans was astounding and by some estimates more than the combined investment in railroads, banks and industries in the North.[77] When the issue of states' rights was raised, the right to preserve the institution of slavery was paramount. Despite the country's abolition of slavery by emancipation through compensation of slave holders, Great Britain's vast textile industry, in which it was estimated that over 20 percent of Britain's population was employed, was fueled by Southern cotton.[78] The South expected Great Britain to come to its aid as an important trade partner, and it did allow the South to purchase munitions and warships. Had Lincoln not seen a way to place support for the South as an untenable option for the British government, Britain could have become a powerful ally for the South.

Just as he had maneuvered the South to being the aggressor at Fort Sumter, Lincoln believed that if he could show the world that it was a war to end slavery more than about what form of government the country would have, he could disrupt any chance of the South gaining recognition from the enlightened foreign nations, particularly those that had fought their own abolition battles. In the summer of 1862, he discussed the concept of emancipation with his cabinet, and in September of that year, he issued a preliminary version of a presidential proclamation to do just that. In a classic carrot-and-stick approach, he offered Southern states the opportunity to rejoin the Union by January 1, 1863, and gradually emancipate their slaves or face immediate emancipation if they did not rejoin the Union. The controversial proclamation puzzled many, and the legality of confiscation of personal property by presidential fiat would have no doubt faced a lengthy congressional debate had it not been framed under the commander in chief's war powers as a military necessity. Some have criticized the document as not emancipating slaves in the border states, over which the president had control, and emancipating slaves in states where he had no power to do so. That argument missed the point. By the stroke of his pen, Lincoln had reframed the war in a manner that set North against South over the issue of slavery and captured the moral high ground. Whatever thoughts the British government had about intervening on the part of the South were thereby doomed in the court of public opinion.

Between the publication of the preliminary emancipation and the final proclamation, the president showed his ability to change course on another issue of major importance to the outcome of the war. His previous objections to the enlistment of African Americans were dropped when, shortly after he issued the preliminary emancipation, he authorized General Rufus Saxton to raise a regiment. "And I further declare and make known, that such persons of suitable condition, will be received into the armed service of the United States to garrison forts, positions, stations, and other places, and to man vessels of all sorts in said service."[79]

General David Hunter, whose previous attempts to emancipate slaves in the Department of the South had been thwarted by Lincoln and whose efforts to form a regiment of African American soldiers were not supported, now had his position reversed when General Rufus Saxton was authorized to raise a volunteer force of not more than five thousand soldiers of African descent on August 25. Saxton's efforts already had seven hundred former slaves under arms on Parris Island by January 1. Lincoln's vacillation on the issue seems to have been on the point of placing armed black troops in the field. He was not opposed to utilizing black recruits for noncombat roles, which accounts for the subtle wording in the emancipation. Perhaps he was too subtle, because others saw it as an open policy to employ black troops in combat. On January 1, 1863, Saxton had the First South Carolina Volunteer Infantry Regiment mustered into U.S. service in Beaufort, South Carolina. The majority of the men of the First South Carolina were formerly enslaved on the liberated South

Carolina and Georgia Sea Islands. He had them sent on an expedition into Confederate-held Georgia and Florida three weeks later.[80]

Several other unauthorized African American units were also mustered into the U.S. military with the enactment of the Emancipation Proclamation. These include three units of the Louisiana Native Guards and the First Kansas Colored Infantry. The Louisiana units, first organized in September 1862, did not serve in combat until May 1863. With the backing of Kansas senator and Union general James Henry Lane, the First Kansas organization began on August 4, 1862, as a state unit.[81] The unit clashed with the Missouri State Guard at Island Mound in western Missouri on October 29, 1862, and drove the Confederates off. The unit lost one white officer and seven men, the first African Americans to die in combat in the Civil War.[82]

Abolitionist governor John A. Andrews of Massachusetts had lobbied with Lincoln to enlist African American soldiers for many months. On January 26, Secretary of War Edwin M. Stanton authorized Andrews to "enlist such companies of artillery and corps of infantry as he may find convenient for a 3 year period and may include persons of African descent organized in separate corps."[83] Before enlisting blacks, Governor Andrews wanted to make sure he could obtain officers of experience and high standing to command a new regiment. He called on Francis Shaw, whose son Robert Gould Shaw Andrews felt would be an ideal colonel. Francis traveled to Virginia, where his son was serving as a captain with the Second Massachusetts Infantry. Robert Shaw telegrammed the governor of his acceptance on February 6, 1863. On February 16, a call was issued for black men to form the Fifty-Fourth Regiment of Massachusetts Volunteers of African Descent. On May 28, the regiment marched through the streets of Boston and onto the steamer *Demolay* bound for Port Royal.

Even before the preliminary emancipation was published, the Confederate government took a very dim view of the arming of slaves. On August 21, general orders were issued condemning General David Hunter for arming freed slaves. The reaction of the Southern leadership to the proposed emancipation and enlistment of African Americans was predictable— it increased their willingness to fight to the bitter end. Not only was the executive action at odds with the private property protections guaranteed by the U.S. and Confederate Constitutions, but arming blacks also struck at the fear of servile insurrection deeply rooted in the Southern psyche. When a Harrisburg, Pennsylvania newspaper pointed this out shortly after the preliminary emancipation was published, Union authorities seized the presses and imprisoned the publisher and owner as treasonous.[84] With the

Colonel Robert Gould Shaw (pictured May 1, 1863) was twenty-five when he led his regiment of black soldiers into the most heavily defended part of Battery Wagner. *Courtesy of the Boston Athenaeum.*

unofficial African American regiments of General David Hunter spread among the Sea Islands of South Carolina and Georgia, it was only a matter of time before someone was captured by Confederate raiders. In November 1862, General Hugh Mercer's raiders captured four armed African Americans in "abolition" uniforms on St. Catherines Island, Georgia, whom he considered slaves with arms in hand against their masters, and he wrote to Beauregard's chief of staff that he recommended making an example of the four with a swift and terrible punishment to deter others.[85] Jefferson Davis made it clear that any slave captured in arms should be delivered over to the respective state authorities to be dealt with according to state law.[86] On May 1, 1863, the Confederate Congress approved a joint resolution on retaliation for the emancipation's enlistment clauses. It provided that Negroes or mulattoes engaged in war or in arms against the Confederate states would be delivered to the state or states where they were captured to be dealt with by the laws of the states. It went further to state that any white person captured commanding, organizing or aiding Negroes or mulattoes in arms against the Confederate states would be declared to be inciting servile insurrection and subject to execution at the discretion of a military court.[87] Delivering these prisoners to the states for adjudication was tantamount to summary execution. Laws directed at containing servile insurrection dated back to before the formation of the United States. A South Carolina law traced back to 1740 mandated the death penalty for attempting to or inciting an insurrection.[88] New York City, which in 1741 was second only to Charleston in slave population, found itself gripped in a servile insurrection known as the "Negro Plot." Following on the heels of an insurrection twenty years earlier resulting in the death of twenty black conspirators, the reaction was particularly brutal, with thirty blacks either hanged or burned at the stake.[89] A similar number were hanged in Charleston in the Denmark Vesey insurrection in 1834.[90] Where slavery existed, the potential for insurrection was real, and most slave states had codes or laws mandating capital punishment for persons convicted of servile insurrection. The incident at Harpers Ferry just seventeen months before the Civil War began resulted in John Brown and his slave conspirators being tried under Virginia's insurrection law and sentenced to death. Ironically, one of the blacks hung was Shields Green, who was born into slavery in Charleston, South Carolina, and escaped to the North, reportedly with the aid of a ship's crew member. In Boston, he became acquainted with Frederick Douglass. Douglass introduced Shields to John Brown.[91]

Chapter 4

A New Plan of Defense

General Beauregard's Return to Charleston

When General Beauregard stepped off the train that carried him from Mobile to Charleston on September 13, 1862, his accolades as the victor in the battle for Fort Sumter and field commander at First Manassas had been tarnished by battlefield reversals and a growing enmity with Jefferson Davis.[92] Not even a petition from forty-nine members of the Confederate Congress was able to sway Davis to change his assignment of Beauregard to the defensive post at Charleston.[93] Whatever personal feeling he may have had with the new command, Charlestonians were delighted to have their beloved hero of Fort Sumter back.

The challenges facing Beauregard on his return to Charleston were daunting. Eighteen months earlier, he had held the upper hand with superiority in men and materiel over the beleaguered Federal garrison at Fort Sumter. Now, the Union had mobilized. Charleston was under blockade, and a foothold carved out of South Carolina at Port Royal provided a base for operations against Charleston and Savannah. Adding to the threat from the Union presence along the coast, Richmond was drawing men from Charleston at an astounding rate to bolster armies elsewhere, and internal bickering in the Confederate command at Charleston had demoralized the military and civilians alike.[94]

Prior to Pemberton's departure for his new assignment, he took Beauregard on a five-day review of South Carolina and Georgia's coastal defenses. Beauregard was dismayed with what he saw. He knew that without superior forces, he depended on the railroads to bring reinforcements from Savannah and Wilmington to threatened positions; however, to allow time to muster troops and munitions, improved fortifications were needed. He immediately requested (on October 7, 1862) that Major David Bullock Harris, his trusted engineer from earlier campaigns, and Captain John Morris Wampler, a talented topographer and engineer, be moved to Charleston. He got Major Harris, but it would take almost a year for Captain Wampler to be reassigned to Charleston.[95]

Beauregard and Harris were an outstanding team of military engineers. Beauregard trusted and respected Harris implicitly and felt that Harris knew instinctively what he wanted.[96] Though Beauregard and Harris were responsible for defenses along the entire South Carolina, Georgia and Florida coasts, it was at Charleston that their plans would have their most severe test. The port city faced the threat of direct naval action and invasion overland from a number of landing points north and south of the city.

What Beauregard and Harris found on Morris Island was woefully inadequate to defend the island or protect Fort Sumter. They were particularly concerned with the new battery under construction near the lazaretto. Work began on the new battery in May, and by September 16, 1862, when Beauregard visited the works, he was told about two weeks were necessary for 577 workmen to complete the project.[97] It was reported that the work contained some armament even at that early date—namely, two rifled thirty-two pounders on naval carriages, two thirty-two pounder smoothbores on barbette carriages and a rifled twenty-four pounder on a siege carriage.[98]

The sand ramparts of the original work were 11–12 feet above high water and extended in a southwesterly direction at a diagonal to the beach to connect with the marsh intrusion that narrowed the island to 280 feet at high tide. Intended for eleven guns, it appears to have been designed strictly as a field work to protect against a land assault from the south, as opposed to a fortified battery capable of sustaining a prolonged siege from land and sea. Beauregard described it as open to the rear.[99] The unnamed work began to be known as the enfilade battery or as the Neck Battery, as Beauregard referred to it.[100] Whatever its state of completion, Beauregard considered that "grave errors" had been made by the engineers in designing and erecting fortifications around Charleston.[101] A particular concern was the absence of protection from enfilading fire from the shipping channel. This was a specific fault of the works he found under construction on Morris Island—he noted that there were no guns bearing on the channel.[102] On his return to Charleston, General Roswell Ripley was asked by Beauregard to estimate his troop need. Ripley identified the Morris Island works as the enfilade battery and that one additional company of artillerists (one hundred men) was needed for Morris Island's defense.[103] On November 4, 1862, General Beauregard officially named it Battery Wagner in honor of Colonel Thomas M. Wagner of the First South Carolina Artillery, who had been killed in the accidental bursting of a rifled gun during a drill at Fort Moultrie on July 17, 1862.[104]

To correct the principal deficiency against attack by sea, Beauregard ordered both increased offensive and defensive capabilities for the battery. Incorporating part of the old ramparts paralleling the sea face, three enclosed gun positions were constructed bearing on the shipping channel. Intervening galleries were created by constructing rooms built like log cabins that were then covered in sand and sandbags. The rooms could serve as ready magazines for the heavy guns in the adjoining chambers. The central room was used as the headquarters. On the southern corner of the sea face, he had a raised bastion constructed to command the beach and protect the land faces of the battery from assault by infantry.[105] For the protection of the garrison, a massive earth-covered bombproof was designed connecting with the rear of the sea face gun chambers. Construction of the bombproof began by laying large wooden grade beams into the sand to spread the load of tons of sandbags covering the roof above the reinforced wooden structure. Reports vary on the capacity of the bombproof, but it was large enough to provide protection for six hundred soldiers.[106]

While this work was being completed, a more expansive plan for defending the island was taking shape.[107] Beauregard's strategy for defending Morris Island consisted of a major remodeling of Battery Wagner, the addition of a supporting battery at Cummings Point (Battery Gregg) and a series of nine detached batteries along the south end of the island. He also called for batteries on Black Island, located in the marsh between Morris Island and James Island, to bear on Lighthouse Inlet, 2.1 miles away. Fort Johnson, at 2.25 miles, and Fort Moultrie, at almost 2 miles, could reach Wagner with their guns but could not be counted on for accurate fire. Fort Sumter was 2,600 yards from Wagner and could fire over the battery but not without endangering the garrison. An additional battery built on the hull of an old ship was begun in the marsh at the entrance of Vincent's Creek to cover the rear of Wagner and the Cummings Point battery.

Beauregard knew he did not have adequate troops to garrison all the points from which Charleston could be attacked and gave considerable attention to how he could quickly reinforce threatened positions.[108] Morris

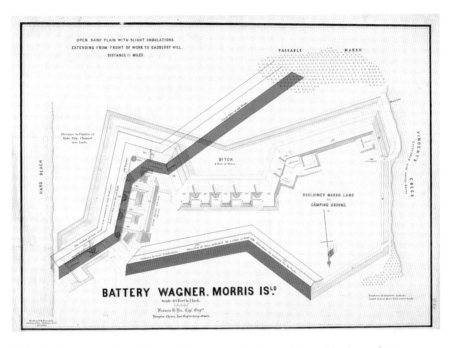

This drawing, prepared by Francis D. Lee, shows the lines of the original open battery. *Courtesy of Harvard University; lines of old work highlighted by author.*

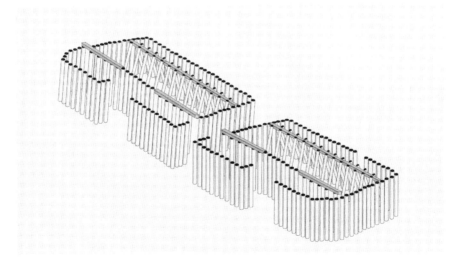

Perspective view of the main bombproof. It was a substantial structure but could hardly hold one thousand men, as General Gillmore reported. *Author's illustration, based on period plans.*

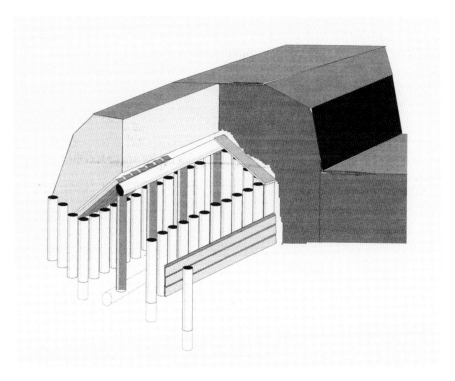

A cutaway view of the powder magazine at Battery Wagner. Timbers were erected on buried grade beams to support tons of sand. *Author's illustration, based on period plans.*

Charleston artist William Aiken worked as a cartographer. His map of Morris Island details the topography of the island. *Courtesy of NOAA Historical Map & Chart Collection.*

Island, separated from James Island by two to three miles of salt marsh and tidal creeks, was dependent on small boats or steamers for reinforcement. In an effort to speed reinforcement, Beauregard had his engineers design a bridge from James Island over Lighthouse Creek to connect with a footpath through the marshes from Black Island to the back side of Morris Island. Where the bridge crossed marshes, it was four feet wide, and over the narrow waterways, it was six feet wide. He also had scouts probe the marshes for trails that could be used at low tide for reinforcements and established rope ferries across the intervening tidal creeks.

Chapter 5

IRONCLAD ATTACK

General Roswell Ripley and General Beauregard at Odds

W hile Beauregard was preparing his defenses, the Union navy was developing a bold strategy for capturing Charleston. Though first seen in the Civil War at Charleston, Lieutenant J.R. Hamilton's railroad-ironclad floating battery concept had been developed five years earlier in the Crimean War. It was but a small step to envision providing such batteries with steam engines. Unable to complete with the U.S. Navy, the Confederacy was forced to innovate and seized on the idea of converting the captured steamer *Merrimack* into an ironclad warship; the eight-month project began in July 1861. Gifted engineer and inventor John M. Brooke contributed to the design. Brooke was an 1847 graduate of the U.S. Naval Academy whose sounding device was instrumental in development of the transatlantic cable. Brooke was awarded a Confederate States of America patent for the design of the CSS *Virginia*, though he was inspired in his innovation by a model developed by John Luke Porter, a former U.S. Navy shipbuilder.[109] Brooke's most significant contribution to the war effort was the large-caliber rifled gun that bore his name. Brooke was not a practitioner of artillery design, but he was a quick study. Inspired by naval ordnance designer John A. Dahlgren's 3.75-inch rifle, he attempted to design a shell for smoothbore cannons that would spin on firing, and by early September 1861, he was experimenting with a rifled projectile.[110] A month later, he determined to put 7-inch rifled guns of his design on pivot mounts fore and aft on the *Merrimack*.[111] Working with the Tredegar Iron Works in Richmond, Brooke designed and had fabricated two 7-inch and two 6.4-inch rifles for

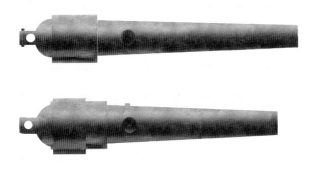

Two of the best rifled cannons of the Civil War. The Parrott weighed 9,700 pounds. The Brooke, eleven inches shorter, weighed 10,700. They could fire 6.4-inch, 100-pound projectiles over five miles. *Courtesy of the author.*

the *Virginia*. The first 7-inch was cast on November 2 and bored and sent to Norfolk to be banded a week later.[112] Brooke's successful rifle design would find many uses on land and sea. Although they had significant range, Brooke saw them as ironclad destroyers more adapted for brief, close-quarter, maximum-charge, armor-piercing applications rather than prolonged long-range firing. Two 7-inch Brooke rifles on center-pintle mounts were added to Fort Sumter's barbette guns after they proved successful on the *Virginia*.

Rumors and reports from spies about the Confederate work on the ironclad created a great deal of concern in Washington, even fears the vessel would steam up the Potomac and demand the surrender of the city. On August 7, the same day the army contracted for seven Eads river ironclads, the navy requested proposals for its own ironclad to be submitted in a month. Fortunately, Swedish American inventor John Ericsson was betting on the government purchasing his ironclad and signed contracts for the iron and hull on October 25; he was already building the engines before the contract was signed. Although Ericsson received most of the credit for the design, the revolving turret was the invention of Theodore Ruggles Timby, who had conceived of the design 20 years earlier.[113] This likely accounts for the speed at which the innovative craft was built—only 118 days. It was commissioned the *Monitor* on February 26 and was towed and steamed to the Chesapeake, nearly sinking on the way. It clashed with the *Virginia* on March 9 off Hampton Roads and effectively ended the *Virginia*'s predation on wooden warships. On February 13, 1862, almost seven months after the Confederates began the *Virginia* project, President Lincoln signed into law HR 153, an act authorizing the construction of twenty steam-powered ironclad gunboats.[114] The act did not specify the design to be employed, as several ironclad concepts were being explored. On February 21, 1862, a contract was let to John Ericsson to build more of them. In April 1862, Admiral David Farragut, in wooden ships, fought his way past Forts Jackson and St. Philips and quickly captured New Orleans. Confident with the success of the Ericsson monitor, the U.S. Navy proposed using the new ironclad ships to run by the harbor forts and force the surrender of Charleston. It began to build a fleet and assemble it at Port Royal.[115]

The Confederates were aware of the operation when the navy began moving the ironclads down the coast. Two days out of Hampton Roads, the original *Monitor* foundered in a storm and sank on December 31 with a loss of four officers and twelve crewmen. The ironclad *Passaic* almost met the same fate on the journey, certainly an inauspicious beginning. The secretary of the Confederate navy, Stephen Mallory, wrote to Lieutenant William A. Webb, on special duty at Charleston, very detailed instructions on February 19 on preparing a fleet of small boats to board the monitors with ladders with a party of ten or twenty sailors, dropping powder charges down the smokestacks, driving iron wedges between the turret and the deck to disable it and smoking the crews out with burning sulfur. The plan was to hold these small boats behind Fort Sumter should the ironclads run past the forts.[116] There was another card in the defense of the harbor: the torpedo, known today as a mine. Escaped slave Allen Davis reported that General Ripley had placed hundreds of these devices in the waters around Charleston by the spring of 1862. Although reports are sketchy, Captain James Christmas Ives, an engineer on Robert E. Lee's staff, appears to have been providing mines about that time.[117] The Confederacy recognized the importance of torpedoes early in the war and formed a naval torpedo service in July 1861 under Commander Matthew Fontaine Maury. Maury's group perfected the electronic denotation variant of the torpedo, but due to a shortage of insulated wire, it planted friction primer devices in the James River in October 1861.[118] The concept of torpedoes was promoted in Charleston and Savannah by Robert E. Lee. As early as February 1862, a U.S. Navy ship discovered torpedoes in the Mud River, a tributary of the Savannah River, that had been placed by Lee's engineer Ives. Later, the Department of Submarine Defenses was organized in Charleston—fifty to sixty officers and men prepared, located, inspected and maintained the torpedoes in Charleston Harbor, while the bureau at Richmond provided skilled labor.[119] In 1863, Gabriel Rains brought his considerable experience with subterranean or land mines to harbor defense, as did Charleston's own Francis Lee. Lee took the idea further and envisioned attacking ships with spar-mounted torpedoes that would detonate on impact. Beauregard was very interested in Lee's concept and recommended that the War Department fund the development.

While Francis Lee proposed a torpedo ram on a surface vessel, other inventors conceived of a semi-submersible, steam-powered craft shaped like a cigar with tapered ends. These little vessels were named Davids, a biblical reference to the giant killer. One of them attacked the most powerful ironclad in the navy. In New Orleans and later Mobile, Alabama, Horace Hunley was working on his idea for a submarine powered by electric motors. When they could not generate the power he needed, Hunley reverted to a crank-powered propeller. Hunley's concept was to either drag a towed torpedo into the hull of a ship or, later, to impale a triggered torpedo into the hull and back off before pulling the lanyard. On the *Hunley*'s final and successful but fatal patrol, it was equipped with a Lee spar torpedo that exploded against the hull of the *Housatonic*. Another effective but difficult-to-maintain defense against propeller-driven ships was a boom of ropes and logs stretched between the west end of Sullivan's Island and Fort Sumter.[120] The harbor tides played fits with the mile-long contraption, and a simpler rope obstruction with stringers was developed.[121]

Just as the Union recognized the potential for ironclad ships, the Confederacy began a program of building ironclads in the wake of the battle between the *Monitor* and *Virginia*. Some, like the ill-fated *Atlanta*, were built on existing ship hulls, but a program of purpose-built, shallow-draft ironclads was also initiated. Charleston quickly launched the *Chicora* and *Palmetto State*. The *Chicora* was funded by the State of South Carolina and the *Palmetto State* by the Confederate government. Both were configured as rams, capable of driving their iron bows into wooden ships. In the early hours of January 31, they attacked and drove off the fleet of wooden blockade ships. Attacking wooden ships was clearly the forte of the Confederate design, but they were no match for the firepower of the Union monitors, as was shown in June 1863, when the *Atlanta* met two of them in the Wassaw Sound near Savannah. Built like the *Virginia* on the hull of an oceangoing ship, it grounded in the shallow sound. A monitor closed to within two hundred yards, and its fifteen-inch shot smashed through the plate armor and wood backing, sending deadly splinters into the gun deck. Another shot took the iron-plated top off the pilothouse, severely injuring its occupants. There was no choice but to surrender.[122] This lesson would have been learned earlier had the Charleston rams engaged Du Pont's monitors. Future designs would incorporate up to six inches of armor over oak.

By April 1863, Admiral Samuel F. Du Pont had seven Ericsson single-turret monitors named after New England rivers; one ironclad with two fixed turrets, the *Keokuk;* and an iron-armored ship, the *New Ironsides*, ready to assault Charleston. To assist the navy, Major General David Hunter ferried seven regiments to the Stono Inlet and occupied Folly Island.[123] The ironclad ships were an impressive array of new technology and forerunners of modern naval ships. They were of composite construction, with wooden hulls and their topsides of wood covered with cast-iron plates held together with rivets. The Ericsson turret design took the ironclad a step further and was composed of free-standing layers of iron plates with a total thickness of eleven inches. The most heavily armed vessel in terms of the number of guns was the *New Ironsides*. It mounted seven eleven-inch Dahlgren smoothbores per side and two eight-inch Parrott rifles fore and aft and was protected by an ironclad belt covering the steeply sloping sides. Iron shutters protected the gun crews when the guns were being serviced, and the ship was piloted during battle from an ironclad pilothouse. The improved Ericsson monitors, known as the Passaic class, each had a fifteen-inch Dahlgren gun matched with an eleven-inch Dahlgren, the one exception being the *Patapsco*, which had an eight-inch Parrott rifle in lieu of the eleven-inch Dahlgren. The fifteen-inch Dahlgren was the largest smoothbore weapon used in the Civil War but, due to a miscalculation, could not fit through the gun port in the rotating turret. An adapter box was designed, but the crew could not see the target and was forced to use the eleven-inch gun to aim the fifteen-inch gun. As opposed to the deck-mounted pilothouse of the original monitor, the Passaic class had a pilothouse that sat on a pedestal running through the revolving turret. The *Keokuk*, with twin fixed turrets, had moveable eleven-inch Dahlgren smoothbores that could fire through one of three gun ports. At 3:00 p.m. on April 7, the fleet steamed up the Charleston channel with the lead monitor, *Weehawken*, pushing an apparatus designed to clear torpedoes. It was one of the largest assemblies of firepower to date. Instead of attempting to run by the forts into the inner harbor, the fleet attacked the harbor forts and was quickly defeated. The Confederates scored a remarkable 439 hits to only 35 by the navy in the artillery duel fought at one half to one mile.[124] According to General Beauregard, this success was due in part to a special device he had asked Colonel Joseph A. Yates to adapt to the heavy guns. This was a crank arrangement that allowed the gun to be traversed or swung smoothly to follow the moving ironclads. It was patented by Colonel Yates in Britain and was known as the Yates traverser.[125] During the run up the channel, Battery Wagner's single rifled thirty-two pounder fired 22 rounds using 132 pounds of powder before an ammunition chest exploded.[126] The explosion at Battery Wagner killed three and injured five. However, the thirty-two pounder was unlikely to do much more than annoy the ironclads.[127] This was not a particularly good day for Battery Wagner. An electrically detonated torpedo of Maury's design had recently been placed half a mile off of the battery and a mile from Fort Sumter. The mine contained 3,000 pounds of blasting powder and was three feet in diameter by eighteen feet long. The huge torpedo and its four anchors weighed 20,500 pounds. As the men were paying out the cable to shore, the boat lost power and drifted on the tide toward Fort Sumter. By the time they got the cable to Battery Wagner, they had paid out two miles of cable, almost twice what they planned. The detonator was a spark gap device packed with fulminating powder set with a 3/32-inch gap. With the *New Ironsides* directly over the device, repeated attempts to explode it failed. There was speculation that the cable had been cut by a wagon wheel on the beach, but tests proved the cable to be intact. The most reasonable explanation is that the spark gap was too large for the length of cable between the batteries and the fuse.[128] Whatever the cause, the *New Ironsides* escaped destruction that afternoon. The ironclads proved difficult to maneuver in the tides and had a very slow rate of fire.[129]

The *New Ironsides* and the *Passaic*-class monitors threw over six hundred tons of solid and explosive rounds into Battery Wagner during the summer of 1863. *From* The Official Records of the Union and Confederate Navies in the War of the Rebellion, *Series 1, Vol. 14 (Washington, D.C.: Government Printing Office, 1902), 596; USS* New Ironsides *by Gutekunst, courtesy of Wikimedia Commons Foundation.*

Admiral Du Pont brought the navy's newest ironclads against Fort Sumter and was defeated. *From Benjamin La Bree and James P. Boyd, eds.,* Official and Illustrated War Record *(Washington, D.C.: Marcus J. Wright and Edward J. Stanley, 1898).*

The *Keokuk,* piloted by Robert Smalls of *Planter* fame, moved in close to Fort Sumter. In a remarkable display of accuracy, a seven-inch Brooke rifle from Fort Sumter placed its first shot through the embrasure of the *Keokuk,* lying nine hundred yards off the fort. The second round hit just above the first.[130] The *Keokuk* took an estimated ninety hits before withdrawing to the front of Morris Island. It was so damaged that the vessel's pumps could not keep up with the leaks, and it sank the next morning without loss of life. Its two eleven-inch Dahlgren guns were recovered by the Confederates within a month, and one was mounted at Fort Sumter.[131] It was reported to Admiral Du Pont that five of the eight ships were damaged to the point that they could no longer use their guns.[132] Though the ironclads withdrew to Port Royal for repairs, the army left recently promoted Brigadier General Israel Vodges in charge of a brigade entrenched on Folly Island and Coles Island.[133] Vodges was a West Point graduate and an experienced artillery officer.[134] With the navy's withdrawal and the rest of General Truman Seymour's troops back in Port Royal, he not unexpectedly wanted to build batteries to protect his small number of troops from the forces in Charleston. They were ordered to keep a low profile so as not to attract attention.[135]

Chapter 6

GENERAL QUINCY GILLMORE AND PRESIDENT LINCOLN SCHEME

Gillmore Prepares His Expedition and Dahlgren Selected

Resident Abraham Lincoln and his cabinet were focused on a quick victory and believed that capturing Charleston would dash the hopes of the Confederacy. Lincoln was disappointed but not surprised by the navy's failure to capture Charleston. He had hoped that with the new iron ships, Du Pont would have steamed by the harbor defenses and demanded Charleston's surrender as had been done at New Orleans. The secretary of the navy had the same hopes and was not pleased that Du Pont determined to fight it out with the forts. Lincoln amplified to Hunter and Du Pont that they must look like they were going to attack Charleston whether they could or could not accomplish that objective.[136] Now that the wind had been taken from the navy's sails, other strategies for capturing Charleston would be entertained.

One of Major Robert Anderson's Fort Sumter officers, Truman Seymour, was now on David Hunter's staff at Port Royal. The artistic Seymour, who gave us detailed sketches of Morris Island, had built an impressive résumé of combat experience, including both battles at Manassas, Malvern Hill and Antietam. He was not afraid of a fight and made up for any timidity that Hunter had about engaging the enemy. Some say it was Seymour who floated the idea of placing Fort Sumter under siege from Morris Island, but proposing and executing are two different matters. On May 11, Hunter wrote general-in-chief of the armies Henry Halleck proposing that if the navy suppressed the Confederate batteries at Lighthouse Inlet, he would plant one hundred– and two hundred–pound Parrott rifles that had recently arrived in Hilton Head on Cummings Point and reduce Fort Sumter.[137] In the execution is where experience counts, and when it came to reducing masonry forts, only one voice could bring experience, Quincy Adams Gillmore. The bee to reduce Fort Sumter was certainly in his bonnet, and while on sick leave in New York City from his command in Kentucky, he began lobbying for the opportunity. How he knew or met the outspoken *New York Tribune* editor Horace Greeley is not known. Some have suggested that Lincoln orchestrated the entire process.[138] On May 23, 1863, Greeley wrote the president's personal secretary, Nicolas Lay, and told him that Gillmore wanted to take Charleston and would "take care of Fort Sumter in three days." Greeley urged Lay that Lincoln should invite Gillmore to Washington by telegraph.[139] To cover his tracks, Gillmore wrote Cullum to remind Halleck of his December 1861 plan the same day.[140] At the request of Greeley, a meeting was held with Lincoln and General Quincy Gillmore. Given Gillmore's success against Fort Pulaski and his desire for action, Lincoln abruptly replaced David Hunter with Gillmore. Before departing for South Carolina, Quincy Gillmore went on a shopping trip to secure some telescopic rifles and Requa batteries, which fired volleys of twenty-five minié balls at the same time.[141] He assumed command from Hunter on June 12.[142] Lincoln turned his attention to finding a bolder admiral to support Gillmore's operations.[143]

Lincoln's selection of a naval leader was no less controversial. Secretary of the Navy Gideon Welles favored Admiral Andrew Foote, but Lincoln wanted his friend Rear Admiral John Dahlgren, commandant of the Washington Navy Yard, appointed. Foote fell ill before leaving for Port Royal and died on June 26 of kidney disease in New York.[144] On June 24, John Dahlgren was ordered to the post of commander of the South Atlantic Blockading Squadron, a position he had long lobbied for.[145]

Despite Beauregard's ambitious plans for Morris Island's defense, outside of Battery Wagner and the Cummings Point Battery (later Battery Gregg), little had been completed at the time of the ironclad attack. Even South Carolina governor Milledge L. Bonham noted the deficiencies and need for additional slave resources in his tour of the island in April, after the attack.[146] Clearly, with the enemy occupying Folly Island, Beauregard suspected another operation would ensue. What he really feared was another assault across James Island like Hunter had attempted the year before and actually considered that a descent on Morris Island would be a "piece of folly."[147]

Beauregard's massive effort to bolster Charleston's defenses had stretched his engineering resources thin, and the lack of progress on the Morris Island

Two of America's most gifted military engineers, Quincy A. Gillmore *(left)* and Gustave T. Beauregard, collided on Morris Island. *Courtesy of the Library of Congress.*

Admiral Samuel F. Du Pont *(left)* and his successor, John Dahlgren, failed to penetrate Charleston's defenses with their new ironclad ships. *Courtesy of the Library of Congress.*

works rankled General Ripley.[148] On June 5, Langdon Cheves reported to Colonel Harris that his work detail of Twenty-First South Carolina soldiers had been commandeered by First South Carolina Artillery captain John Mitchell, who under direct orders of General Ripley was attempting to complete the works on the south end of Morris Island on his own.[149] As late as May 1863, two of the nine guns intended had not been mounted, and none of the supporting magazines, shelters and hospitals had been constructed. Cheves had his workmen finishing a "small but important" part of Battery Wagner.[150] Ripley reported that the main magazine for the detached batteries was complete on June 14 and that the guns had been supplied with ammunition.[151] Four of the guns were arranged to cover the crossing at the inlet, and a line of rifle pits had been extended on a spit of land known as Oyster Point that also bore on the inlet.

The only bright spot in the defense arrangements of Morris Island was Battery Wagner. Under Cheves's leadership, a much stronger work emerged. In addition to its sea face armament, the land face and rear, facing Cummings Point, saw major changes.[152] From the raised bastion on the southeast corner, the battery's wall indented, allowing four gun positions bearing down the beach with high traverses between them to protect them from enfilading fire

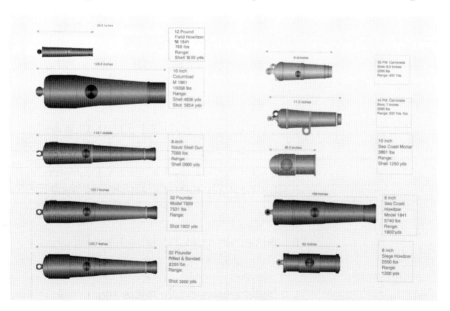

Battery Wagner mounted an array of armament. The smaller pieces were antipersonnel weapons. The larger and rifled pieces bore on the shipping channel. *Author's illustration.*

from the shipping channel. This area, known as the curtain, was protected by a moat that could be flooded with several feet of water and by flanking cannons on the bastions and western wall where it extended southward to create the indent. A large powder magazine was built into the extending wall. The guns along these walls, unlike the sea face armament that fired *en barbette* or over the parapets, were protected by firing through narrow embrasures lined with palmetto logs to keep sand from falling in. These embrasures could be closed with sandbags for protection of the guns until needed. The land face parapet now stretched 630 feet from the sea to the bay and the sea-facing parapet 210 feet from north to south, enclosing an area of roughly three acres.[153]

By connecting an existing ridge of sand dunes, the battery was enclosed to its rear and along Vincent's Creek by a lower parapet. A banquet, or step for soldiers to mount for firing over the parapet, was built of wood along the wall. Within the parade stood a number of lightly constructed wooden quarters and storehouses.[154] Entrance to the fort was via a small opening onto Vincent's Creek and a larger sally port on the northeast corner. Outside the sally port, a gun platform for field pieces was raised perpendicular to the sea face from which the face could be raked with canister and grapeshot and shells could be directed down the beach to the south. To hold the fine quartz sand in place, both sandbags and sod mats cut from marsh grass were used.[155]

Chapter 7

THE JULY 10, 1863 AMPHIBIOUS LANDING ON MORRIS ISLAND AND THE FIRST ASSAULT ON BATTERY WAGNER, JULY 11, 1863

General Quincy Gillmore had assured the president that he would capture Morris Island, lay siege to Fort Sumter as he had Fort Pulaski and pave the way for the Union navy to enter the harbor and demand the surrender of the city. His new command consisted of about twenty thousand effective troops holding positions from St. Augustine to Folly Island. He determined that he could commit twelve thousand troops to the Charleston operation and, about the middle of June, began ferrying men and materiel from Port Royal to Folly Island, immediately to the south of Morris Island, where a regiment had been encamped since the ironclad attack.[156] The remoteness of Folly Island and lack of Confederate coverage of Stono Inlet made Folly an ideal staging area for his expedition against Charleston. Transport and supply ships could land on the southern end of the island, where a landing had been constructed. Confederate lookouts and scouts could see the troop movements on the remote island but could do little to stop them.

The presence of three regiments of African American troops among his forces at Port Royal made no impression upon Gillmore, and they were not included in his plans for the grand assault. This did not sit well with Colonel Robert Shaw, left behind in his camp in Beaufort. There is no evidence that Gillmore and Shaw knew each other, but Shaw had an important ally in Gillmore's command, Major General George C. Strong. The two New England natives had become reacquainted on the Fifty-Fourth's arrival at Beaufort. Shaw wrote Strong to request that the Fifty-Fourth be included in the assault. Strong intervened, and the Fifty-Fourth arrived on Folly Island in time to be part of diversionary actions.

The first order of business for Gillmore was to get his troops on Morris Island, and the weak and unfinished Confederate defenses at Lighthouse Inlet gave him an opening. In late June, he began developing plans to ferry troops across the inlet from behind Folly Island while using naval and land artillery fire to suppress the detached batteries. He planned to create a diversion by feigning an attack on James Island at the same time. To get his land batteries as close as possible without disclosing his intentions, he constructed batteries on the northern end of Folly Island behind a stand of trees. Because access to this area was across a barren strip of land, this work had to be conducted at night. Gillmore set up his headquarters on Folly Island on July 8, 1863.[157] The south end of Morris was very difficult to defend. It was much broader than Cummings Point and was out of the effective range of the harbor forts. Reinforcements, supplies and ammunition had to be moved almost three miles along the exposed beach and across the dunes from the landings communicating with the city. The south end was open to the ocean at the shipping channel, and it was an easy target for naval operations. Further, none of the guns installed in the sand hills were capable of damaging ironclad ships. The Twenty-First South Carolina Infantry, 350 strong, dug in with rifle pits along Oyster Point fronting the inlet and waited.

To draw Beauregard's attention away from Morris Island, Gillmore landed troops under Brigadier General Alfred Terry on James Island on the afternoon of July 8 and loaded his men into a collection of small boats in the Folly River. The men sat in the boats all night when the assault was canceled due to bad weather. Unfortunately, his batteries had been partially unmasked and were discovered by the Confederates.[158] The next night, they repeated the process, and at midnight on the high tide, they began the slow journey through the creeks leading to Lighthouse Inlet. During the night, Gillmore finished unmasking his batteries, and at 5:10 a.m. on the morning of July 10, 1863, they began firing on the Confederate positions in the sand hills. The navy brought four ironclads into action about an hour later standing just off the southern end of the island. The ill-prepared batteries were no match for the overwhelming firepower that could be heard miles away. About 9:00 a.m., Gillmore began ferrying his troops across Lighthouse Inlet.[159] The boat assault split into two arms, one engaging the Confederate infantry while the other skirted east of Oyster Point and landed closer to the ocean under the protection of the bank afforded by low tide. Seeing that they were about to be cut off, what remained of the Twenty-First South Carolina Infantry and the artillery detachments withdrew to Battery Wagner with the Union troops and ironclads in pursuit. The ironclads steamed offshore, keeping pace with the troops. As the ironclads began to fire at Battery Wagner at about 9:30 a.m., a fragment from one of the first rounds penetrated an open gallery where Langdon Cheves was working at his desk, struck him in the head and killed him instantly.[160]

As soon as the retreating Confederates cleared the field of fire, Battery Wagner opened its land face guns on the assaulting troops.[161] With the massive battery looming before them, the Union troops, exhausted from fighting almost three miles up the island in the blazing heat of the noonday sun, halted their assault. In the words of one of the attackers, "It was clearly demonstrated that the fort was far more formidable than it was supposed to be by the commanding general."[162] The navy learned that day that the battery could pack a punch. Three of the ironclads were hit by Battery Wagner's artillery. The lead ironclad, with Admiral Dahlgren aboard, received sixty hits; a large percentage of them were deemed severe by the admiral.[163]

While he nervously watched troop movements on the Stono River and James Island, on the afternoon of July 10, Beauregard ferried Colonel Charles Hart Olmstead's 534 effectives, newly arrived from Georgia, to assist Colonel Robert F. Graham's battered Twenty-First in garrisoning Battery Wagner.[164] At that point, the battery had a contingent of 1,770 infantry and artillery and was ready for what was to come in the morning.[165]

Without consulting Admiral Dahlgren, Gillmore ordered his battle-tested troops to assault Battery Wagner at dawn. The brigade-strength attack on the battery by seasoned Union infantry was a singular disaster. In the course of a few minutes, a third of the attacking regiment was killed, wounded or captured. Confederate losses were fewer than twenty of the garrison. Requesting naval support to prevent a Confederate counterattack, Gillmore told Dahlgren that he did not think it "well" to make another assault.[166]

The Confederates deployed another weapon that day that was not seen by the Union forces. Captain Martin Gray of the torpedo service in Charleston deployed fifty-seven explosive shells buried in the sand from fifty to sixty feet in front of the moat. Equipped with pressure-sensitive fuses, they would detonate if a person stepped on the hidden trigger.[167]

Chapter 8

The Union Brings in Heavy Artillery

Confederate Preparations and Reinforcements, July 18, 1863

Chastened but not discouraged, Gillmore believed his artillery could batter Battery Wagner into submission, and after hastily establishing a defensive line across the island just north of the Beacon House in case the Confederates counterattacked, he began building artillery batteries to lay siege to the earthwork.[168] He had available to him at the time for siege purposes five two hundred–pounder Parrott rifles, nine one hundred–pounder Parrott rifles and thirty mortars from small three hundred–pound, 5.8-inch Coehorns up to seventeen thousand–pound, 13-inch siege mortars.[169] He asked the navy to engage Battery Wagner during the day to suppress fire against his works.[170] Two lines, or parallels, were constructed, one 1,350 yards from Battery Wagner and another to the west at 1,830 yards.[171] Forts Sumter and Moultrie, firing at 2.25 to 2.75 miles, respectively, were not effective in stopping Gillmore's engineers.[172] On July 15, Gillmore moved his headquarters to Morris Island from Folly Island.[173] After originally scheduling another assault on July 16 and ordering General Terry to withdraw from James Island, he rescheduled for the 17th. Finally, on July 18, he was ready. Then a torrential rainstorm delayed the start of this next attempt at capturing the battery.[174] Around 9:00 in the morning and continuing at a steady pace until about noon, five gunboats engaged Battery Wagner with ten guns at long range. During this time, Gillmore replaced rain-soaked powder for his batteries. The entire ironclad fleet was then brought into range, and shortly after 12:30 p.m., forty land-based guns and twenty-seven naval guns began one of the most intense artillery barrages of the Civil War. The barrage continued at a furious pace, estimated at twenty shells a minute, until dusk.[175]

Battery Wagner's garrison dismounted and covered its lighter guns with sandbags to protect them during the barrage. Most of the garrison sought protection in the bombproof and sand hills between Batteries Wagner and Gregg. In the July heat with little ventilation, this was a trial. Ordnance lieutenant colonel John Mallet recalled that his most memorable experience of the war was the suffocating interior of the sandbag bombproof at Wagner.[176] To guard against a sudden rush, the Charleston Battalion maintained its post on the parapets under galling fire. The wooden officer's quarters and medical dispensary building in the western parade were literally obliterated by artillery shells.[177] About 4:00 p.m., on the high tide, the monitors moved to within three hundred yards of Wagner, and in a short period, most of the battery's sea face guns were silenced.[178]

During the day, Gillmore had General Truman Seymour arrange almost six thousand men in three brigades along the southern shore of Morris Island. Although he believed only one brigade would be necessary, the second was instructed to be ready to immediately support the first, while the third was placed in reserve. Included in the reserves was an African American regiment, the Second South Carolina Volunteer Infantry. Unlike the Fifty-Fourth, recruited as educated freemen, the Second South Carolina was recruited from former slaves on the Sea Islands of South Carolina, Georgia and Florida. The unit began forming in March 1863 and mustered into service on May 22, 1863, with Colonel James Montgomery as the commander. The unit, along with the Fifty-Fourth Massachusetts, had participated in the burning of Darien, Georgia. A more notable action of the unit was the Combahee Raid, which liberated seven hundred slaves from the rice plantations. The unit had little training relative to the rest of the brigade. Some of the units had been in formation since 10:00 a.m., and when assembled, the line stretched almost a mile.[179] The head of the line was near the Beacon House. The assault was to begin at dusk in order to reduce the impact of Confederate artillery, but timing was critical to avoid a risky night operation.

The Fifty-Fourth Massachusetts, leaving about one hundred men behind to guard its camp on St. Helena Island at Port Royal, arrived in the Stono Inlet about noon on July 9. Two days later, the men landed on James Island to join General Terry's diversion. They were picketed near the site of the Secessionville battle when, on July 16, Confederates under Brigadier General Johnson Hagood attacked and captured fourteen soldiers of the Fifty-Fourth

This Haas and Peale image from the late summer of 1863 shows Union troops occupying the Beacon House. *Courtesy of the Library of Congress.*

who stubbornly held their ground, allowing a Connecticut regiment time to withdraw.[180] The engagement became known as the Battle of Grimball's Landing. That night, Terry received orders to evacuate James Island. Some of the units went by transports and others on a two-and-a-half-mile trek across marshy ground at night.[181] The Fifty-Fourth and the Second South Carolina were among those making the journey through the rain. While awaiting transport to Folly from Cole's Island, Shaw received orders late on July 17 to report to General George C. Strong on Morris Island without delay. It would take him almost eighteen hours to move the regiment about seven miles. About 4:30 in the afternoon, Robert Shaw and the Fifty-Fourth Massachusetts arrived from their journey through the marshes of James Island; ferry transit across the Folly River; march north along Folly Island; and ferry transit across Lighthouse Inlet. There can be no doubt that their presence on Morris Island had not been planned as part of the operation by General Seymour. What happened next is equally as providential. The only general officer that Shaw knew on the island was George C. Strong, and Strong was in charge of the lead brigade. Strong agreed to assign the Fifty-Fourth to the lead position, which had been known in similar assaults as the "forlorn hope." It was the role of the forlorn hope to occupy the fort's defenders in hand-to-hand combat while following regiments swept over the defenses. It meant that the unit would be severely tested and would have many casualties. Some newspaper accounts indicated that General Seymour thought the unit expendable, but it is hard to imagine that the entire assault would be risked by placing a unit in the lead that would not engage the enemy.[182] Further, in his official report of the action, he stated that the Fifty-Fourth Massachusetts was a well-officered unit of excellent character.[183] The first brigade, commanded by General George C. Strong, was ordered to advance with the bayonet only, rifles loaded but not capped to prevent stopping to fire and reload.[184]

Opposing the Fifty-Fourth were close to 1,700 Confederate infantry and artillerists garrisoning Battery Wagner. These consisted of South Carolina, North Carolina and Georgia units. Many had been brought by rail from Savannah and Wilmington the week before. The battery was under the direct command of General William Taliaferro.

The brigade was advised to deploy as a column of regiments when it neared the works. A deployed regiment was the common mode of assault during the Civil War and consisted of ten companies across in two ranks. The Fifty-Fourth, at 650 effectives, was larger than the other regiments and deployed in two wings of five companies. Shaw led the first wing, and his friend Lieutenant Colonel Edward N. Hallowell led the second. As the artillery fire ceased, Shaw advanced his men down the beach. They had to cover over one thousand yards to reach the battery. Even with the double wing formation, the companies on the right, B and E, were forced to march knee deep in the ocean where the beach narrowed before the battery.[185] The rest of the first brigade waited until Shaw reached Battery Wagner before beginning its advance. By the time the rest of the brigade started, Shaw and the Fifty-Fourth were within rifle range of Battery Wagner, and a hail of bullets caused the unit to stop momentarily. The flag bearer went down, and Sergeant William Carney picked up the colors. Shaw got the unit moving again and directed his first wing into the ditch in front of the curtain wall where the battery was indented between the sea face bastion and the land face bastion. The point of assault chosen by Shaw was the most strongly defended in the entire battery, where the Fifty-First North Carolina Infantry, under Colonel Hector McKethan, had been positioned by General William Taliaferro. Ironically, the sea face and bastion were essentially undefended, because the Thirty-First North Carolina Infantry, which had been assigned to defend the positions, would not come out of the safety of the bombproof.[186] This left only about 700 men in a position to defend the entire battery and was a major factor in what little success was gained in the assault. Another

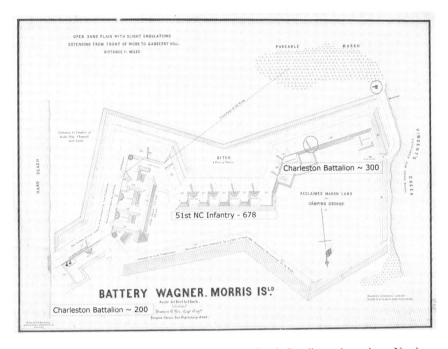

On July 18, 1863, defending troops consisted of two South Carolina units and two North Carolina regiments along with artillery detachments from Georgia and South Carolina. The Thirty-First North Carolina refused to take its posts on the seafront. *Courtesy of Harvard University; highlighting by the author.*

factor in the success of the Fifty-Fourth reaching the battery was the state of the battery's land face guns. In the curtain, only one of the eight-inch naval guns was functional during the assault.[187] A thirty-two pounder to the west of the curtain, directly under the flag, only fired two rounds before being put out of order. The defenders in that section were able to bring a twelve-pound howitzer to fire into the flank of the Fifty-Fourth as it crossed the ditch. This piece fired eight loads of grape and canister at point-blank range and caused massive destruction in the attacking regiment.[188] For twenty long minutes, the remnant of the Fifty-Fourth battled alone against the garrison's defenders until General Strong and the balance of the first brigade reached the battery. Some of the inexperienced Fifty-Fourth Massachusetts men broke and ran down the beach through the oncoming regiments.[189] Others clambered up the walls into the undefended bastion. Lieutenant Colonel Hallowell led the second wing into the bastion to Shaw's right. Most of the survivors were in the second wing.[190] When the Sixth Connecticut Infantry and Forty-Eighth New York Infantry reached the battery, they passed along

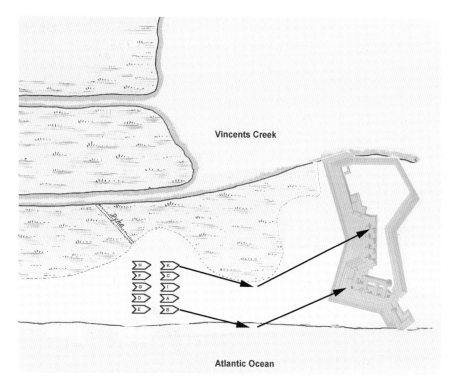

Vincents Creek

Atlantic Ocean

The Fifty-Fourth Massachusetts broke into two wings, the first led by Colonel Shaw and the second by Lieutenant Colonel Hallowell. The star marks where Shaw died. *From Louis F. Emilio,* History of the 54th Massachusetts Volunteer Infantry, 1863–1865 *(Boston: Boston Book Company, 1894); formation illustrated by the author.*

the undefended sea face and occupied the gun positions protected from the garrison by the high walls of the bombproof.

The first brigade had gained a foothold in Battery Wagner and expected that the second brigade would bring much needed reinforcements. But the second brigade, which had been unexpectedly halted near the Beacon House, did not advance as planned.[191] Messengers were sent a mile to the rear by General Seymour to urgently request support. Colonel Halimand Putman, second brigade commander, reported that General Gillmore, who watched the battle from the top of an observation platform almost a mile away on Gregg's Hill, had given him orders not to advance.[192] Taking his own initiative, Putman got his New Hampshire, New York and Ohio regiments moving, but by that time, it was totally dark, and the first brigade, fighting for over twenty-five minutes, had sustained heavy losses. To make matters worse, the approaching units, unable to distinguish friend from foe, fired into the backs of the regiment ahead of them. Colonel George B. Dandy of the One Hundredth New York Infantry reported that the companies assigned to follow the Fifty-Fourth Massachusetts into the curtain found it impossible to do so.[193] Instead of a single coordinated assault, it was as if the battle had stopped and restarted, and the advantage of the first wave had been lost.[194] Generals Strong and Seymour were wounded, but Seymour ordered the reserve brigade up. With panicked, discouraged and wounded men pouring back through the lines, General Gillmore ordered his chief of staff, Colonel John Turner, to take command of the third brigade and countermand Seymour's order.

The decision to abort another assault was prudent, because Colonel George P. Harrison's Thirty-Second Georgia Infantry, 565 strong under Brigadier General Johnson Hagood, had been ordered to Battery Wagner from Fort Johnson to reinforce the garrison.[195] The reinforcements arrived by the steamer *Chesterfield* after the assaults but participated in the recapture of the sea face. By 11:00 p.m., the Confederates had captured and driven all the Union forces from the battery. A survivor who was captured called it "a

Drawing of July 18, 1863 assault from within the battery. Curtain on right. Remains of commissary building on left. *From the* Illustrated London News, *September 1863, courtesy of the Library of Congress.*

butchery, not a battle."[196] The day ended as it began, with Battery Wagner defiantly blocking complete Union control of Morris Island.

Though the narrow approach limited the number of men that could be engaged at one time, the ferocity of the fighting was a match for any battle of the Civil War.[197] The three-hour battle took a severe toll on the lead regiments.[198] Particularly destructive were three twelve-pound howitzers that had been brought to Battery Wagner after the assault on July 11. These short-barreled field pieces acted like giant shotguns and were arranged so that one battery of two fired directly down the beach, while the third piece, mounted by Colonel Harris outside the battery on Vincent's Creek, provided crossing fire.[199] The Fifty-Fourth Massachusetts lost 42 percent killed, wounded and captured; the Forty-Eighth New York, 58 percent; the Sixth Connecticut, 28 percent. In the second brigade, the Seventh New Hampshire lost more officers than any Union regiment in any single battle of the entire Civil War. The unit had 43 percent casualties. General Strong suffered a mortal wound, and General Seymour was carried off the battlefield and out of action for almost three months. Both generals were hit by grapeshot. Colonels Shaw and Putnam died on the parapets. After the battle, Captain Gray found that twenty of his torpedoes had exploded, which may have accounted for the impression that the defenders were throwing hand grenades.[200] These were among the highest casualty rates of any unit engagements in the war. Confederate defenders lost 36 men killed and 135 wounded, and General Beauregard telegraphed his old commander Joseph Johnson, "Praise be to God! The anniversary of Bull Run has been gloriously celebrated."[201]

Chapter 9

The Siege of Wagner and Destruction of Sumter

The Evacuation of Morris Island

After several relatively quiet days, on the morning of July 24, new land batteries five hundred yards closer and the entire naval ironclad fleet began a barrage said to be equal to that of July 18 but focused on the weakest parts of the work. Fortunately, an exchange of prisoners that day brought a four-hour lull in the bombardment. Battery Wagner's commandant, General Taliaferro, took stock of the damage from the artillery barrage. The covering of the principal magazine was at one point exposed to the extent that the supporting timbers were being hit by shells. Taliaferro felt the battery was in danger of being destroyed and sent signals to General Ripley to arrange for evacuation. One of the artillery officers, Captain Charles E. Chichester, strongly disagreed with Taliaferro, asked for permission to go to the city, commandeered a boat and met General Ripley in his headquarters at the Southern Wharf, where he informed him that the battery was fully capable of being defended.[202] Beauregard wrote James Seddon, Confederate secretary of war, that after two unsuccessful assaults, the contest had become purely military engineering dependent on time, labor and long-range guns.[203] To gain time to complete his new defensive works, he needed Battery Wagner held and told Ripley to tell Taliaferro that "the work must be held and fought to the last extremity consonant with legitimate warfare." The Confederates determinedly held the battery for fifty-four days under conditions so terrible as to defy description. In the final days, it became impossible to force slaves to repair the battery.[204]

Morris Island looking north from the Beacon House shows the terrain over which the siege was fought. *1863 Haas and Peale image, courtesy of the Library of Congress; Fort Sumter and Battery Wagner located by the author.*

In response to his request for eight thousand more troops to cover his losses, General H.W. Halleck wrote a scathing letter reprimanding Gillmore for attempting the operation.[205] Gillmore, with Fort Sumter in his sights and Charleston in the distance, realized his plan would require a different approach. He determined to build batteries for his heavy Parrott rifles on sandy ridges extending into the marsh behind Morris Island to bring them as close to Fort Sumter as he could get without capturing Battery Wagner. He also arranged for a detached battery, well into the marsh, that would put Charleston within range. Gillmore determined to prevent the nightly repairs of damage caused by his artillery and ordered Drummond lights to illuminate Battery Wagner and Fort Sumter. He originally intended to mount a light on the bow of a monitor, but the motion of the vessel made this unsatisfactory. He set them up on land a mile from Battery Wagner and employed members of the Fifty-Fourth Massachusetts to help produce the hydrogen gas needed for their operation.

On August 12, Gillmore began preliminary fire against Fort Sumter, noting the effect of the shells. On August 17, at 5:00 a.m., eleven Parrott rifles, soon joined by fire from ironclads, began what would be a seven-day artillery bombardment, at the end of which Gillmore declared Fort Sumter neutralized.[206] To announce his intentions for Charleston, on the night of August 23, he opened his "Swamp Angel," a two-hundred-pounder Parrott rifle, on the city.[207] He used a supply of incendiary material known as Mr. Short's Greek-fire.

Having failed to take Battery Wagner in two direct assaults, Gillmore determined to take the battery by siege work, digging a network of zigzag trenches that, by September 8, stretched almost two miles to the sea face of the battery. To accomplish this massive feat, he ordered General Terry to form a brigade of two thousand Colored Troop soldiers to be used for fatigue duty at the landing at Lighthouse Inlet and on Morris Island.[208] On August 26, General Gillmore ordered General Terry to capture the rifle pits 250 yards in front of Battery Wagner. On duty were eighty-six men of the Sixty-First North Carolina facing an assaulting force of two regiments. Among the captured, according to Corporal James H. Gooding, a black reporter in the ranks of the Fifty-Fourth Massachusetts, were five black men; three were enslaved workers but two were soldiers, fully equipped as Rebel sharpshooters possessing the very best patterned rifles. One of the sharpshooters admitted to owning slaves himself and displayed a proud demeanor.[209] The Fifty-Fourth had encountered, to its dismay, two of the rare black Confederates. The Sixty-First was recruited from several counties in eastern North Carolina. The state had the second-largest population of free blacks in the South, numbering some thirty thousand in the 1860 census.[210]

The effort required to throw up defensive lines, prepare gun batteries, haul heavy artillery, carry tons of supplies from Lighthouse Inlet to the middle of the island and dig miles of entrenchment was among the largest commitments of man-hours in the war. Just to emplace one siege gun against Battery Wagner required 240 man-hours of labor. A heavy breaching cannon against Fort Sumter required 600 man-hours to put in position. The proportion of effort roughly divided 40 percent against Battery Wagner, 25 percent against Fort Sumter, and the balance in the defensive lines. Three-quarters of this work was shoveling sand. All this was accomplished during the hottest months of the year. To keep the troops safe from artillery during off hours, camps were located at the southern end, necessitating a four-mile round trip to the lines, and to minimize loss of life at the front lines, most of the work was done at night.

Major Thomas Benton Brooks provided many revealing details in his engineering reports on the operation. Most revealing is that of the eighteen thousand man-days involved, half of the effort was provided by black troops.[211] The disproportionate share of the burden falling on the blacks resulted in Brooks sending a questionnaire to the engineers who directed the operations. He stated that the effort was an experiment to prove the fitness of the American Negro as a soldier and that never before had such a large burden of fatigue duty fallen on black troops under such hazardous conditions as in the siege of

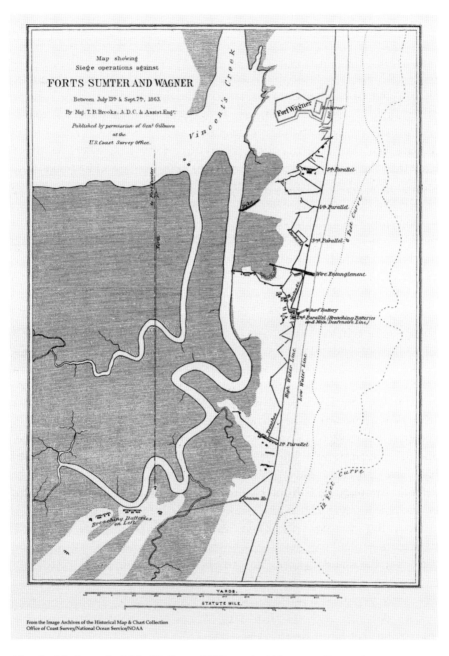

After the failed assault of July 18, General Gillmore had his troops dig trenches to Battery Wagner's sea face. *From* The War of the Rebellion: Atlas to Accompany the Official Records.

Morris Island. He posited five questions regarding courage under fire, quality of work, quantity of work, speed and initiative and, in relation to the first four points, how the regiments recruited from free blacks compared with regiments recruited from slave states.[212] Six officers replied. To the question of courage, all six found the black troops more timid under fire but more willing to follow the example of the officer in charge. They also agreed that the black trooper was less skilled than his white counterpart, but that made little difference in the siege work. All found that the black troops performed a greater quantity of work than the whites by laboring more constantly but that white troops were more enthusiastic and responded better to emergencies. As a final note, Brooks reports that sickness was greater among whites than blacks during the siege.

On September 5, Gillmore turned eighteen mortars and rifled guns against the beleaguered sand battery and was joined by the *New Ironsides* during the daylight with its eight-gun broadside. Within forty-two hours, the army and navy fired 3,500 projectiles at Battery Wagner.[213] On the evening of September 6 and the morning of the following day, while Gillmore arranged his troops for another assault, Beauregard successfully evacuated Batteries Wagner and Gregg with the loss of only forty-six men.[214] Because of the bombardment and the fact that the trenches had almost reached the moat in front of Battery Wagner, most of the trenching was stopped. But engineering Lieutenant Peter Michie noticed that the artillery was so accurate that the head of the trenches was the safest location of all. He found four black soldiers in the fifth parallel and organized them into a working party. They encountered and safely removed six or seven of Captain Gray's torpedoes and then broke through into the trench where the dead of the Fifty-Fourth had been buried.[215] Their brave and grisly work was unnecessary—the defenders were gone. Fortunately for the sappers, the fuse designed to blow up the powder magazine opposite where they were working failed.[216]

From the morning of July 7 until Morris Island was evacuated, Confederates had sustained 1,174 men killed, wounded or captured defending the island.[217] Union casualties for the campaign were 2,318, over half sustained in the failed assault of July 18.[218] An estimated 150 casualties were recorded in the trenching and fatigue work alone.[219]

Both defender and foe alike had labored under conditions that defy description. All faced death daily from artillery and sniper fire. Whether men were manning artillery, repairing and building fortifications or digging trenches, the blazing heat, foul water, decomposing bodies, incessantly blowing sand and insects added to their misery.[220] The U.S. Sanitary Commission, a U.S. government–approved volunteer organization that

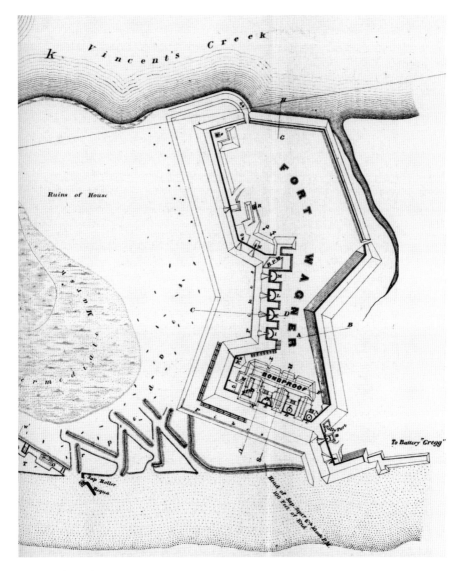

These views of Battery Wagner, prepared by Union engineers after the Confederate evacuation, reflect modifications done during the siege. *Courtesy of the Library of Congress.*

supplied medical and humanitarian aid to soldiers, had an icehouse erected on Lighthouse Inlet to distribute ice to the soldiers.[221] During that summer and fall, the commission provided 390 tons of ice.[222] For the defenders, General Beauregard ordered a cycling of the garrison on a three-day interval, with the relief carrying in their provisions.[223]

Top: This view after the Confederate evacuation shows the destruction caused by almost ten thousand artillery shells. The main bombproof entrance is to the left rear. *Courtesy of the Library of Congress.*

Bottom: *Left to right:* Stephen A. Swails, Peter Vogelsang and Frank M. Welch were sergeants of the Fifty-Fourth Massachusetts and later promoted to lieutenants. *Courtesy of the Smithsonian African American Museum.*

There was no want of valor in the campaign for Morris Island. General Gillmore produced medals to recognize uncommon valor and sent five to each regiment to award as they saw fit. One regiment returned them, saying there were not enough to go around. He also renamed Battery Wagner Fort Strong in honor of his fallen brigade commander. Beauregard recognized five defenders by requesting their names be added to the Confederate Roll of Honor. The efforts of the men of the Confederate Signal Corps were also recognized for their months of hazardous duty carrying signals between Batteries Gregg and Wagner.

Chapter 10

THE NAVAL ATTACK ON SUMTER

The Stalemate Continues, General Foster's Costly Attack on Fort Johnson, Fort Sumter Occupied and the Real Results

With Morris Island in Union hands, rifles and mortars could now be brought to within three-quarters of a mile of Fort Sumter, and much of Charleston would fall within range of Federal artillery. Gillmore and, later, Fort Sumter veteran General John G. Foster expended enormous resources for the next seventeen months bombarding Fort Sumter and Charleston. They would be no closer to capturing the city than when they began. While they rested and resupplied between major bombardments, Confederate engineers used slaves to repair and convert Fort Sumter into a bombproof earthwork that was more capable of resisting attack than at the beginning of the war. Incandescent calcium lights arranged to play on the fort at night were futile at preventing work.[224] So were attempts to capture the fort by small-boat attacks and to destroy it with powder rafts floated on the tide.[225] The final disastrous attempt to advance off of Morris Island was by General Foster. He had replaced Gillmore as commander of the department in May 1864. He organized an assault on Fort Johnson from small boats that was an unmitigated disaster. The night operation involved about 1,000 soldiers setting off from Vincent's Creek. The boats lost their way or grounded in the shallow water and were discovered by Fort Johnson's 130 defenders. Seven of the attackers were killed, 23 were wounded and 140 captured.[226] This does not include 18 enlisted men who drowned when their boat capsized.[227]

Beauregard was no less creative in the use of military technology. After the assault of July 18, he realized that there was no possibility of dislodging the

Federals from Morris Island and began strengthening his mainland defenses. He arranged over twenty cannons to fire on Morris Island from James Island and used balloons for aerial reconnaissance of the Union positions on Morris Island.[228] He also invested in more powerful cannons and torpedo launches to battle with the ironclads, should they enter the inner harbor, and organized a strike force of Confederate marines to board the monitors with ladders to disable them by dropping grenades down their smokestacks. The harbor was extensively mined and obstacles built to force ships to pass key fortifications. By placing strong earthworks along the city waterfront, converting Castle Pinckney into a powerful earthwork, strengthening Fort Johnson and building numerous other batteries, Beauregard turned the entire inner harbor into three zones of overlapping artillery fire.[229]

A serious rift developed between Gillmore and Dahlgren when Dahlgren would not bring his fleet into Charleston Harbor. Dahlgren, not having been party to Gillmore's plan with Lincoln, was content to periodically have his ships trade shots with Confederate fortifications and made no serious attempt to enter the harbor. The boldest action taken by Dahlgren was to order a small-boat attack on Fort Sumter just after midnight on September 9 with about 500 officers and men. Gillmore planned a small-boat attack the same night with two regiments, but neither communicated to the other until twelve hours before the assault.[230] The two argued as to whether the attack was to be led by an army or navy officer. Gillmore called off his attack.[231] Dahlgren should have. The Fort Sumter garrison was prepared and turned the night assault into a disaster, with over 120 officers and men captured.[232] The lack of cooperation between the army and navy was the subject of numerous news articles. Secretary of the Navy Gideon Welles queried Admiral Du Pont in April 1864 as to whether he had even given Dahlgren copies of his orders to fully support Gillmore. Du Pont, no fan of a repeat of his April 7 debacle, equivocated on the point, saying he "abstained from committing" Dahlgren to any specific plan of operations.[233] The tragic loss of the *Patapsco* with 68 of its crew in January 1865 to a torpedo (mine) while probing the water between Forts Sumter and Moultrie was a confirmation of Dahlgren's fears.[234] He so disliked Gillmore that in his journal he considered requesting to be relieved rather than work with the general when he returned to his post in 1865.[235] At the end of the war, Dahlgren made a lengthy documentation of the harbor defenses but affirmed that his hesitance was largely based on the massive effort needed to capture Battery Wagner.[236] His ships, despite bombarding the battery for sixty-three days, had been unable to force capitulation of the work. He knew that if he entered the harbor, where torpedoes were planted like "autumn leaves," he would lose ships and end up having to fight his way back out of the harbor.[237] Gillmore, of course, expended much analysis in diminishing the threats perceived by Dahlgren in his postwar accounts.[238] Even Gillmore admitted that 122,230 pounds of metal had failed to reduce Battery Wagner, while 110,643 pounds of metal had breached Fort Pulaski.[239]

The enmity that existed between Union leaders was not the only fallout over the campaign for Morris Island. Richmond demanded accountability for the loss of the island. General Roswell Ripley was not shy about reporting what he saw in the lead-up to July 10. Unfortunately, in doing, so he impugned his superior. The two battled for the rest of the war and in print for years afterward.[240] At one point near the end of the war, Ripley, looking for a change of command, asked to be sent anywhere Beauregard was not involved. By that time, Ripley's reputation for disagreeing with his superiors was well known, and his wishes were not honored.

In his reflections on the campaign for Morris Island, Beauregard spoke of the defense in grandiose terms—"The defense of Fort Sumter and that of Battery Wagner are looked upon as two of the most skillful, desperate, and glorious achievements of the war. They stand unsurpassed in ancient and modern times."[241] Beauregard boasted that the Union did exactly what he wanted and became trapped in its own success. Possession of the island brought the Union no closer to Charleston than when it attacked Secessionville in July 1862.[242] The Confederate flag was still flying at Fort Sumter on February 17, 1865, when the Confederates evacuated the city rather than be cut off by Major General William Tecumseh Sherman's legions marching through the state. Then, and only then, could Gillmore occupy the city he promised President Lincoln he would capture twenty-one months earlier.

The value of Gillmore's efforts to capture Charleston was questioned during and after the Civil War. For Gillmore himself, the reduction of Fort Sumter and the capture of Morris Island earned him a promotion to major general of volunteers.[243] With the operations at Charleston going nowhere, Gillmore was cycled through several positions before returning to the Department of the South in early February 1865. Barely four months after Gillmore gained control of Morris Island, the captain of the battle-tested ironclad *Weehawken*, John Rodgers, testified before the U.S. Senate on the navy attempting to enter Charleston Harbor: "I do not think the game is worth the candle."[244] Former Confederate general and postwar South Carolina governor Johnson Hagood reflected on the campaign in his memoirs of the war by positing the same question. In Hagood's view, the effort and loss of life in the campaign for Morris Island accomplished little to bring the war to an end.[245] It could be argued that, just as the Union was tied down at Charleston to hold onto its costly gains, Confederate resources were also tied down. The Union forces captured an amazing 450 pieces of ordnance when Charleston was evacuated.[246] The army learned a lot about rifled artillery and the strength of earthworks against it.[247] One foreign observer would write of his experience at Charleston that "modern artillery began there."[248] Certainly the prolonged artillery barrages caused a great part of the city to be vacated, but military headquarters, hospitals, post offices and other essential services were moved out of range and continued to function. On the east side of the city, shells reached as far north as Wragg Square, a distance of five miles from the Cummings Point batteries. Beauregard's headquarters at the nearby Aiken-Rhett House were a target.[249] Both sides housed prisoners in locations exposed to artillery fire in a failed attempt to stop the bombardment.[250] One would have expected that Union occupation of Morris Island would close the port to blockade running, but even this vital source of war materiel, though hindered, was not stopped completely.[251] Almost ninety blockade runners entered the port during the eighteen months of the siege.[252] One blockade runner tried to enter the harbor on February 18, 1865, the day Union forces occupied the evacuated city, and several were captured in port. At first glance, especially in regard to the virtual stalemate at Charleston, the campaign appears to have accomplished little for all the deaths, injuries and expenditures. In Beauregard's words: "The possession of Morris Island and the demolition of Sumter by the Federal land and naval forces, were mere incidents in the drama. These did not cause the fall of the much hated and much coveted rebel city."[253]

The cost of capturing and defending Morris Island in terms of human capital was significant to both sides. As was customary during the war, reports accounted for killed in action, wounded and missing in action. What these categories do not tell is how many of the wounded succumbed to the effects of their wounds or resulting complications such as gangrene or tetanus. From the medical records of the Department of the South, one can determine not only battle casualties but also the impact of the biggest killer of the Civil War—disease. For the period of July, August and September 1863, field hospitals treated 866 cases of gunshot wounds and reported that 122, or 14 percent, had died in hospital from those wounds. During the same period, 198 soldiers died of disease and accidents.[254] While these reports are for the entire department, it was on Morris and Folly that the troops were concentrated. By January 1864, there were approximately 6,000 troops stationed on Morris Island and another 10,000 on Folly.[255] While battle deaths on Morris Island never reached those levels again, deaths from disease continued until the very end. Based on the 1863 data, it can be estimated that an average of 14 soldiers were dying on Morris Island per month from disease alone. Over the span of the campaign, it is likely that in excess of 350 soldiers died from disease acquired on the island, and when added to the 381 killed in action and an estimated 192 who later died of their wounds from the time of the Confederate evacuation, the sailors who died in small boat attacks on Fort Sumter and those who died in the abortive attack on Fort Johnson and other actions in the Charleston area, nearly 1,000 Union men died.[256]

Battle losses of the Confederates on Morris Island were lower because of the protection offered by the defensive works, but even after evacuating the island the bombardment of nearby Confederate defenses took a toll. John Johnson attributed 52 killed and 267 wounded at Fort Sumter during the siege.[257] Not included in Johnson's summary are the enslaved workmen who at times were suffering more from the artillery than the soldiers. Johnson's account suggests that as many as 25 to 30 were killed.[258] Many more were wounded, and a special hospital was established on the southeast corner of Cannon and Spring Streets to care for enslaved men wounded or taken ill at Fort Sumter and other Confederate works.[259] The Confederate soldiers were not immune to the diseases that claimed so many Union troops; even Beauregard's favorite engineer, Colonel D.B. Harris, who assisted in designing Morris Island's defenses, died on October 10, 1864, of yellow fever, which was epidemic in the fall of 1864.[260]

Finding value in the campaign requires looking beyond the battle and toward the war itself. It also requires consideration that slavery, the very cornerstone of the Confederacy as pronounced by Vice President Alexander Stephens, could have contributed to its downfall. Major General Patrick Cleburne and thirteen other Confederate officers in the West saw it coming in January 1864 when they wrote, "Slavery, from being one of our chief sources of strength at the commencement of the war, has now become, in a military point of view, one of our chief sources of weakness."[261] The Militia Act of 1862 and the Emancipation Proclamation had given the U.S. military the opportunity to enlist free blacks and former slaves, but a number of ranking generals thought this unwise.[262] What was needed was a true test of whether the black man would stand and fight. General Strong placing the Fifty-Fourth Massachusetts in the van of his brigade on the evening of the July 18 assault created as severe a test as could be imagined. The people of Massachusetts knew that something of immense importance had happened on Morris Island and published within a year a body of letters and writing on the events. Perhaps one of the most memorable accounts was written by a *New York Post* correspondent who visited some of the nearly two hundred wounded shortly after they arrived in Beaufort. He posited to a large group of the wounded lying with shattered or amputated limbs that getting shot and mangled by artillery was not what they had bargained for to get into the war. Among the many affirmative remarks and readiness to continue the struggle, he heard it said, "If all our people get their freedom we can afford to die."[263]

Confederates in contemporary and postwar accounts made much of the recoil of the unit in the heat of battle. Clearly some men panicked and fled the battlefield, but when Confederate lieutenant Iredell Jones surveyed the scene in front of Battery Wagner the day after the assault, the bodies of the black soldiers piled in the curtain ditch, on the parapets and inside the battery spoke of brave soldiers. Prisoners captured within the battery also bore witness of bravery and determination.[264] On his return to Fort Sumter, he wrote, "The negroes fought gallantly."[265] The fact that brave men of African descent had fought and died before Battery Wagner could not be hidden.[266] As news of the gallantry of the Fifty-Fourth Massachusetts Volunteer Infantry filtered north, it was seen as a sign to the nation that black men were capable soldiers.[267] By year's end, over fifty thousand African Americans had been enlisted in the U.S. Army.[268] Efforts accelerated to recruit almost two hundred thousand African Americans into the Union army and navy, fulfilling Lincoln's goal for the Emancipation Proclamation.[269] By war's end, African Americans, though not yet citizens, made up almost 10 percent of the fighting forces of the Union.[270] Those recruited from liberated slave populations not only added to the Union's ranks, they also represented a loss of the South's manpower to raise crops and build and repair railroads and fortifications. Horace Greeley had little to say about Gillmore's campaign for Morris Island that he had so strongly recommended to Lincoln. However, when the war had come to a close, his newspaper published its conviction that the gallantry of the Fifty-Fourth Massachusetts before Battery Wagner had shortened the war by a year.[271] Viewed not as a failed quest to capture the symbolic heart of the rebellion but for its value in turning the tide of prejudice against black soldiers, the game was "worth the candle."

Chapter 11

REFLECTIONS ON THE AFTERMATH
OF THE WAR

Recognition of Contributions of African Americans, Racial Animus and Morris Island Today

T he sands of Morris Island just to the south of the sand hills closest Lighthouse Inlet became the camp of the Fifty-Fourth Massachusetts until Charleston was evacuated.[272] Other expeditions that involved the Fifty-Fourth included a push by General Gillmore into Florida that culminated in the Battle of Olustee, where again the Fifty-Fourth deported itself bravely and took a number of casualties.[273] The regiment also fought in the Battle of Honey Hill in an attempt to capture the Charleston-to-Savannah railroad to assist General William T. Sherman's advance on Savannah. Part of the regiment remained in the field to assist Sherman's march through South Carolina. The main unit entered Charleston on February 27 and camped in Magnolia Cemetery on the northeast border of the city. While there, the unit was able to retrieve its record books from its old camp on Morris Island. Two weeks later, it was ordered to garrison duty at Savannah. The last action the unit saw was a move to destroy railroad resources in eastern South Carolina in early April, known as Potter's Raid after General Edward E. Potter, who organized it. On April 18, the unit fought its last battle of the war at Boykin's Mill, about twenty-five miles northeast of Columbia.

When the regiment was assembled again in Charleston, it was billeted in the Citadel on Marion Square. The experience the soldiers had with the uneducated, newly freed slaves made a significant impression on them. They had started a collection to recover their fallen commander's body and return it to Boston, but it was proposed that they fund a school for blacks in

Charleston in his name. The regiment raised $2,832, and with additional funds from Shaw's family friends and New England philanthropists, the men funded a school on Mary Street in Charleston known as the Shaw School. This was a sizeable amount of money for men who had refused for eighteen months to accept pay until the government agreed to pay them the same as white soldiers.[274] The structure was a three-story affair, and today, the first floor continues to serve the children of Charleston as a Boys and Girls Club.

While on occupation duty in Charleston, an incident occurred that illustrates the struggle African Americans faced in a white man's army. A great deal of racial animosity existed between white and black units occupying Charleston that summer. On July 9, a unit of the 54th was fired on in the Charleston Market not by Confederates but by Union soldiers, members of the 167th New York Infantry. Privates Charles Porter and Robert Nelson were wounded.[275] General Gillmore investigated the incident and found the New Yorkers at fault. He had the unit's flags removed and the regiment placed under arrest in Fort Wagner.[276] Gillmore, in an attempt to reduce racial conflict, withdrew the black regiments from the cities and began to discharge those units raised in the North. In August 1865, the 54th Massachusetts was relieved from garrison duty and ferried to Mount Pleasant, on the eastern shore of Charleston Harbor, and assembled to be mustered out of the service on August 20. Most of the unit then boarded transports back to Boston, where it was greeted on September 2 by throngs of well-wishers as it paraded through the streets.[277]

A handful of Fifty-Fourth Massachusetts veterans remained in Charleston following the war. At least two of the unit found romantic interests in the city. Isaac Sawyer, a private in the unit who enlisted from Burlington, Vermont, at the age of nineteen, met his future wife, Rachel Morant. They married at the Centenary Methodist Church in Charleston and raised a family while he worked as a barber in the city. Isaac died of natural causes on July 19, 1893, thirty years and a day from the assault on Battery Wagner. He is buried in the Monrovia Cemetery. His last barbershop was at 252 King Street, near the intersection with Hasell Street. The Hayden and Whilden building next door housed the offices of the Corps of Engineers in charge of constructing Fort Sumter in 1860.

Lieutenant Stephen Atkins Swails also met and married a Charleston native, Susan Aspinall. Susan lived on Henrietta Street one block from the old Citadel, where the Fifty-Fourth was billeted. Stephen was a ferry operator in Elmira, New York, when he enlisted. Older than the average recruit, he became a sergeant in the unit and was at Shaw's side when Shaw died on the parapets of Battery Wagner. In recognition of his bravery and leadership, Swails was the first African American promoted from the field to an officer grade. Other African Americans had received officer rank, such as Major Martin Delany, but were direct commissions based on prewar status. Sergeants Peter Vogelsang and Frank Welch were also commissioned from the field, but their commission were only approved just before the regiment was mustered out.[278] Lieutenant Swails was wounded at Olustee and during Potter's Raid, when one of his own men mistook him for a train engineer.[279] Stephen Swails's leadership skills and bravery served him well following the war. He became a lawyer and trustee of the University of South Carolina, served as the mayor of Kingstree, South Carolina, and was a two-term senator in the South Carolina Legislature, where he was president pro tempore. The image of a land with liberty and justice for all proved to be fleeting. Swails's leadership was a threat to the white Southern establishment, which was disenfranchised following the surrender of the Confederacy. South Carolina was an occupied state chafing under a government of elected black representatives who shaped a new constitution embracing civil rights for the emancipated. The old guard resorted to what it knew to be a tried and true method for controlling the black population. For over two hundred years, Southern men had been schooled in the techniques of controlling the enslaved. The view that slavery operated by physical restraints ignores the impracticality of working in chains. The "peculiar institution" depended on the enslaved producing valuable work unfettered by chains and locks. Certainly there was the potential for withholding what little pleasures might have been allowed to keep the slaves hard at work, but a much greater hold was inculcated fear. No slave was punished in isolation—spectacles were made so that all could see the violence that would be meted out for attempting to escape or for disobeying the master's orders. Slavery was a culture of fear beginning at an early age. It was to fear and intimidation that the Reconstruction-era South turned, only this time it was to oppress the freedman. Beatings, murders and lynchings were the tools, and voting statistics measured the results.[280] Prior to the Civil War, only six states allowed black men to vote, and none was a slave state.[281] Having ended slavery, the Fifteenth Amendment to the Constitution guaranteed the right to vote for the black male. In South Carolina under military occupation, black representatives passed a new constitution that mandated political equality without regard to race in 1868. The progressive constitution was replaced in 1895 with a vastly more racially biased foundational document that practically disenfranchised black voters for the next sixty years. In

South Carolina, black voter registration decreased from 92,081 in 1876 to 2,823 in 1898.[282] The growing danger of reprisal to black leaders forced Swails to leave South Carolina for a government position in Washington, D.C. He remained in Washington until, in ill health, he returned to his wife and children in Kingstree, where he died in 1900. His wife had his remains returned to Charleston and buried at the Humane and Friendly Society Cemetery, just outside of the gates of Magnolia Cemetery, near where he had encamped among the tombstones when he first entered Charleston. In 2006, the African American Historical Alliance, with the assistance of the people of South Carolina, erected a monument on his unmarked gravesite.

The intrepid Robert Smalls, whose knowledge of the defenses had inspired the attack on Secessionville, continued to serve U.S. efforts throughout the war aboard the steamer he knew so well. As was the custom in the navy, he and the crew of the *Planter* were awarded prize money.[283] Smalls's $1,500 reward enabled him to return to Beaufort, the place of his birth, and purchase the house where he grew up. He even provided support for his former owner's wife in her old age. After the war, he entered state politics, and when South Carolina was readmitted, he became the U.S. congressional representative from the Beaufort district. The disenfranchisement of black voters ended his political career, and he served as U.S. customs collector for Beaufort until 1911. Smalls died in 1919 and is buried in his hometown. In 2012, on the 150th anniversary of the date he commandeered the *Planter*, the Historic Charleston Foundation and African American Historical Alliance placed a marker on the Charleston Battery near the location of the Southern Wharf, where his journey to freedom began. Robert's descendants unveiled the monument. The City of Charleston placed a marker in Waterfront Park near the site of the Northern Wharf, where he rescued his family from slavery on the same date.

The soldiers of the Fifty-Fourth who were captured at James Island on July 16, 1863, and at Battery Wagner on July 18 presented a significant problem for General Beauregard and the Confederate authorities. The wounded were transported to a hospital on Queen Street in Charleston, while the prisoners were temporarily housed at Castle Pinckney. The soldiers in Castle Pinckney told their captors that they would abide by South Carolina law and were willing to work on Confederate batteries.[284] This may have been in an effort to avoid the death penalty they had been threatened with. Beauregard soon learned that a number of the Fifty-Fourth claimed that they were freemen. He appealed to Richmond for an answer as to how to handle the situation.[285] Secretary of War James Seddon responded that all Negroes captured in arms should be turned over to the state authorities, making no distinction of free or slave.[286] In accordance with the Confederate orders, South Carolina governor Milledge Bonham demanded that those members of the Fifty-Fourth Massachusetts who were slaves be released to the state and appealed to the War Department for disposition of the freemen.[287] He then wrote the secretary of war informing him of an 1805 South Carolina statue that any person who aided a slave in insurrection should be tried and put to death.[288] Even the medical department was confused as to how to treat the black wounded and had not provided clothing to some of the soldiers. Beauregard's adjutant advised the surgeon in charge that due attention should be provided to the men.[289] The secretary of war wrote Bonham on August 1 that all the Negro prisoners should be turned over to the State of South Carolina.[290] Bonham wrote ten days later that he would hold to trial those slaves and freemen from Southern states and defer action on those from Northern states. Secretary Seddon submitted the recommendation to President Davis, who advised not bringing any case to trial and stated that he was unsure of the powers of the governor to do so.[291] The prisoners were then moved to the Charleston Jail while awaiting a resolution on their fate. The situation was now squarely in Bonham's camp. Seddon wrote Bonham urging him to postpone bringing any Union Negro soldier to trial or to exercise his powers to execute such persons, warning him of the possibility of Federal retaliation against white prisoners.[292] In all the confusion, Bonham determined to bring 4 members of the Fifty-Fourth to trial who were suspected of being former slaves. The three-day trial was held in August with the soldiers being represented by two outstanding attorneys, Mitchell Nelson and Edward McCrady. It was held in the Charleston County Courthouse, which still stands on the corner of Meeting and Broad Streets, and ended with the decision that the courts had no standing in the matter.[293] The accused were sent back to the Charleston Jail, where all the prisoners were held in limbo until December 1864, when they were turned over to the Confederate military and relocated to the Florence Stockade, a twenty-three-acre prisoner-of-war camp about fifty miles north of Charleston with about 7,500 other prisoners. Those who did not perish there were shuttled by train to North Carolina as Sherman approached. They were exchanged on parole on March 4, 1865, in Goldsboro, North Carolina. While in the Florence Stockade or immediately after release, 14 soldiers died—a mortality rate almost four times that of the eighteen-month interment at the Charleston Jail.[294] The treatment of these and other black soldiers captured during the war and the South's refusal to exchange black prisoners led to a suspension of the policy of prisoner exchange.[295] Although the nonexchange policy contributed greatly to the suffering and deaths of soldiers on both sides of the conflict, it can be argued that the impact on Southern armies was greater due to its ever decreasing pool of manpower.

Almost six months after the Fifty-Fourth was mustered out in Mount Pleasant, the First South Carolina Volunteer Infantry, which had been reconstituted as the Thirty-Third U.S. Colored Troops and headquartered in Battery Wagner in the fall of 1865, was assembled on the beach in front of the battery for its own mustering out. Standing as near as could be determined to the grave of Colonel Robert Shaw and forty of his fallen men, Colonel Charles Trowbridge reminded the unit of what had occurred at that site and of its importance to African American heritage. He said, "Near you rest the bones of comrade Shaw, buried by an enemy's hand in the grave with his black soldiers who fell by his side, where in the future your children's children will come on pilgrimages to do homage to the ashes of those that fell in this glorious struggle."[296]

In 1897, the State of Massachusetts honored the unit by erecting a magnificent bas-relief bronze monument designed by Augustus Saint-Gaudens on Boston Common. It reflects Robert Gould Shaw leading the unit off to war from the grounds where their journey to Morris Island began. In attendance at the unveiling was Sergeant William Harvey Carney. Born a slave in Norfolk, Virginia, his freedom had been purchased by his father, who escaped to Massachusetts. Carney picked up the unit's colors and carried them onto the parapet of Battery Wagner, where he became a conspicuous target. He suffered three gunshot wounds before crawling off the battlefield with the flag. Carney was awarded the Medal of Honor for his bravery before Battery Wagner in 1900. After surviving the deadly curtain of Battery Wagner, at which so many of his comrades perished, he died in 1908 from injuries suffered in an elevator accident at the Massachusetts State House, where he was working as a messenger.[297] Massachusetts governor Roger Wolcott made perhaps the most memorable speech at the dedication, saying, "Fort Wagner marked an epoch in the history of a race, and called it into manhood."[298]

The City of Charleston unveiled a bronze plaque on the sesquicentennial of the assault on Battery Wagner in recognition of the event at a gathering at White Point Garden. Because of ongoing construction to repair the seawall, the plaque could not be mounted where it was intended. Finally, in December 2015, the plaque was mounted in the sidewalk of the High Battery near the grand Confederate defenders monument. It overlooks Fort Sumter in the

William Harvey Carney saved the Fifty-Fourth Massachusetts's colors in front of Battery Wagner and was wounded three times. Here he is photographed by James E. Reed about 1901–8 wearing his Congressional Medal of Honor. *Courtesy of Moorland-Spingarn Research Center, Howard University.*

The site of Battery Wagner is mostly underwater. A) western parapet; B) rear wall; C) curtain; D) sea face bastion. *Image by the author, 1996.*

distance. While not so grand as Boston's Saint-Gaudens monument, it is a step in the right direction.

While the legend of the Fifty-Fourth Massachusetts is alive and immortalized in monuments, film and print, Morris Island bears little resemblance to the battleground of 1863.[299] Described as one great graveyard in 1864, not even the dead were left in peace as the island began washing away and exposing their bones.[300] It was observed during the siege of Battery Wagner that the island was losing a foot a day to the sea.[301] By 1878, Battery Gregg at Cummings Point was being washed into the sea.[302] Two years later, work began on the system of rock jetties to open the shipping channel directly to sea. The south jetty landed on the beach at a point just north of Battery Wagner. Erosion of the island accelerated greatly during this period, and by 1883, so much of the beach had eroded that the jetty had to be extended shoreward another 513 feet.[303] Battery Wagner was still recognizable in April 1884 when visited by a veteran of the Forty-Eighth New York.[304] Within a month, the site was surveyed by three former Confederate defenders of the battery, who reported not a trace of the battery or any the Union's siege works remained.[305] The southern end of the island has been particularly susceptible to erosion and has pivoted in a westerly direction. The lighthouse erected in 1876 to replace the one destroyed by the Confederates was sited well inland from the ocean, near where the camps of the Fifty-Fourth Massachusetts were located. Today, that lighthouse is surrounded by the Atlantic Ocean; the shoreline is almost a third of a mile away. If current projections for sea level increase are realized, before long, the entire island will be gone. It is hoped that the memory of what transpired on that island during the Civil War and how it changed this nation will live on.

NOTES

Introduction

1. George Cullum, "Annual Report of Operations to Light House Board, Oct. 20, 1857," *Fort Sumter Letter Book* (Charleston Museum), 33; Joseph A. Yates, report, November 27, 1863, in *The War of Rebellion: A Compilation of the Official Records of the Union and Confederate Armies*, Series 1, Vol. 28, Part 1 (Washington, D.C.: Government Printing Office, 1890), 531 (hereafter cited as *ORA*); William H. Campbell, journal of operations, April 25, 1864, in *ORA*, Series 1, Vol. 35, Part 1 (Washington: Government Printing Office, 1891), 176. During part of the war, the house was the headquarters of Colonel Robert F. Graham of the Twenty-First South Carolina Infantry and was called Graham's House by the Confederates. This structure was torn down by Union soldiers in 1864.
2. "Items and Incidents," *Army Navy News*, September 5, 1863: 19.
3. Report of State Officers, Board and Committees to the General Assembly of South Carolina (1879), 627, 862. In 1857, the State of South Carolina enacted a bill for using Morris Island as a lazaretto. It resumed after the war as a lazaretto under the care of the City of Charleston.
4. William J. Neal et al., *Living with the South Carolina Shore* (Durham: Duke University Press, 1984), 6–7, 95.

Chapter 1

5. Special Correspondent from Port Royal, "Arrival of Five Escaped Slaves," *New York Times*, December 16, 1862. While only a few injuries were reported among the garrison, no deaths were reported on either side. However, an escaped slave reported to a *New York Times* correspondent that after the battle he was sent to bail water out of Lieutenant John R. Hamilton's floating battery, which had grounded near the southwest tip of Sullivan's Island. There he found three mangled bodies that apparently had gone unnoticed. Major Anderson specifically fired at the ironclad battery, and it is possible that in the confusion of the battle, men could have gone missing and not been reported as casualties.

6. Margaret L. Coit, *John C. Calhoun: American Portrait* (New York: Houghton Mifflin, 1950), 171.

7. Lincoln's first inaugural address; he referred to the Corwin Amendment, adopted by Congress, unnecessarily signed by President Buchanan, and forwarded to the states, whether seceded or not, for ratification under Lincoln's signature. The amendment would protect the right of a state to condone slavery within its borders in perpetuity and unamendably. This is known as the "ghost amendment," as it was not fully ratified before the Civil War. Only Kentucky, Ohio, Rhode Island, Maryland and Illinois ratified it. Most amendments were not numbered before ratification in recognition that the states might not approve them, but confident that Corwin's amendment would pass, it was prematurely called the Thirteenth Amendment. The number was later given to the amendment abolishing slavery, ratified on December 6, 1865, almost eight months after Lincoln's assassination. The abolition of slavery in U.S. territories was not accomplished until new treaties could be executed with Native American tribes not bound by the U.S. Constitution and its amendments. This process was completed on June 14, 1866.

8. David Flavel Jamison to Lewis Melvin Hatch, January 17, 1861, in *ORA*, Series 1, Vol. 53 (Washington, D.C.: Government Printing Office, 1898), 120.

9. Lincoln wrote the expedition's planner, Gustavus Fox, thanking him and acknowledging that the outcome (either peaceful reinforcement or casus belli) was in the best interest of the nation.

10. Montgomery Blair to Abraham Lincoln, March 15, 1861, in *ORA*, Series 1, Vol. 53, 63–64.

11. Heath L. Pemberton Jr., *Fort Sumter: Chronological Construction History with Architectural Detail* (Charleston, SC: Fort Sumter National Monument, 1959), 54.

12. Fitz John Porter to Samuel Cooper, November 11, 1860, in *ORA*, Series 1, Vol. 1 (Washington, D.C.: Government Printing Office, 1880), 72.

13. Robert W. Barnwell, James H. Adams and James L. Orr to James Buchanan, December 28, 1860, in *ORA*, Series 1, Vol. 1, 109–10.

14. Robert Anderson to Samuel Cooper, January 6, 1861, in *ORA*, Series 1, Vol. 1, 133.

15. Alfred Roman, *The Military Operations of General Beauregard in the War Between the States, 1861 to 1865* (New York: Harper, 1884), 1:37.

16. Charles Dew, *Apostles of Disunion: Southern Secession Commissioners and the Causes of the Civil War* (Charlottesville: University of Virginia Press, 2001), 38.

17. Roman, *Military Operations*, 1:31.

18. Wilmot G. DeSaussure, orders, no. 93, March 29, 1861, in the Wilmot G. DeSaussure Order-Book 3330-z, Southern Historical Collection, Wilson Library, University of North Carolina at Chapel Hill.

19. John G. Foster to Joseph G. Totten, April 5, 1861, in *ORA*, Series 1, Vol. 1, 242–44.

20. "A Night in the Harbor," *Charleston Mercury*, April 15, 1861.

21. *Charleston Daily Courier*, April 13, 1861.

22. Warren Ripley, *Artillery and Ammunition of the Civil War* (Charleston, SC: The Battery Press, 1970), 274–75.

23. Robert Lebby, "The First Shot on Fort Sumter," *South Carolina Historical and Genealogical Magazine* 12, no. 3 (July 1911):141–145; Wade Hampton Gibbes, "First Shot in the War," *Southern Historical Society Papers* 31 (1904): 73–79.

24. Wade Hampton Gibbes Jr. "William Hampton Gibbes, No. 1874, Class of 1860," *Thirty-Fifth Annual Reunion of the Association of the Graduates of the United States Military Academy* (June 14, 1904).

25. "Statistical Report of Shots Fired from Every Battery," *Charleston Mercury*, May 5, 1861.

26. W.A. Swanberg, *First Blood: The Story of Fort Sumter* (New York: Dorset Press, 1957), 327.

27. James Chester, "The First Scenes of the Civil War Concluded by Captain James Chester Third US Artillery," *United Service: A Monthly Review of Military and Naval Affairs* 10, no. 6 (June 1884): 616–29.

28. Robert Wilson Gibbes, report no. 27, in *ORA*, Series 1, Vol. 1, 66.

29. John G. Foster, report no. 7, October 1, 1861, in *ORA*, Series 1, Vol. 1, 24.

Chapter 2

30. Gustave T. Beauregard to William Henry C. Whiting, April 16, 1861, in *ORA*, Series 1, Vol. 53, 147.

31. Gustave T. Beauregard to Leroy Walker, April 21, 1861, in *ORA*, Series 1, Vol. 53, 152.

32. Gustave T. Beauregard to Ambrose Gonzales, April 22, 1861, in *ORA*, Series 1, Vol. 53, 153.

33. Antonio Rafael de la Cova, *Cuban Confederate Colonel* (Columbia: University of South Carolina Press, 2003), 142.

34. Ibid., 155–56.

35. John R. Waddy, general orders 26, June 9, 1862, in *ORA*, Series 1, Vol. 14 (Washington, D.C.: Government Printing Office, 1885), 556.

36. Gustave T. Beauregard to Francis Pickens, May 16, 1861, in *ORA*, Series 1, Vol. 53: 167-68.

37. Charles Oscar Paullin, "President Lincoln and the Navy," *American Historical Review* 14, no. 2 (January 1909): 284.

38. Ezra J. Warner, *Generals in Gray: Lives of the Confederate Commanders* (Baton Rouge: Louisiana State University Press, 1959), 309–10.

39. Walter Edgars, ed., *South Carolina Encyclopedia* (Columbia: University of South Carolina Press, 2006), 510.

40. Arthur Peronneau Ford and Marion Jonstone Ford, *Life in the Confederate Army Being the Personal Experiences of a Private Soldier in the Confederate Army, and Some Experiences and Sketches of Southern Life* (New York: Neale Publishing, 1905), 27; Gustave T. Beauregard, "Torpedo Service in the Harbor and Water Defences of Charleston," *Southern Historical Society Papers* 5, no. 4 (1878): 154.

41. Francis W. Pickens to Jefferson Davis, January 7, 1862, in *ORA*, Series 1, Vol. 6 (Washington, D.C.: Government Printing Office, 1882), 366.

42. "Lighthouse Blown Up," *Charleston Mercury*, December 20, 1861.

43. Charles Henry Davis to Flag Officer Samuel F. Du Pont, December 21, 1861, in *Official Records of the Union and Confederate Navies in the War of the Rebellion*, Series 1, Vol. 12 (Washington, D.C.: Government Printing Office, 1901), 422 (hereafter cited as *ORN*).

44. George W. Cullum, Entry 859, *Biographical Register of the Officers and Graduates of the U.S. Military Academy at West Point, N.Y., from Its Establishment, March 16, 1802 to the Army Reorganization of 1866–67* (New York: J. Miller, 1879), 1:502–03; Paul L. Hedron, "On Duty at Fort Ridgely Minnesota, 1853–1867," *South Dakota State Historical Society* 7, no. 2 (1977): 9.

45. Thomas W. Sherman to General McClellan, December 26, 1861, in *ORA*, Series 1, Vol. 15 (Washington, D.C.: Government Printing Office, 1886), 211–13.

46. James C. Hazlett, *Field Artillery Weapons of the Civil War* (Urbana: University of Illinois Press, 2004), 109.

47. Michael B. Ballard, "Wrong Job, Wrong Place: John C. Pemberton's Civil War," *Journal of Mississippi History*, Special Civil War Edition (Winter 2013), 3–9.

48. David Hunter, general orders no. 1, March 31, 1862, in *ORA*, Series 1, Vol. 6, 257–58.

49. Herbert M. Schiller, *Sumter Is Avenged: The Siege and Reduction of Fort Pulaski* (Shippensburg, PA: White Mane Publishing, 1995), 82–83.

50. Quincy A. Gillmore, *Official Report to the Engineer Department on the Siege and Reduction of Fort Pulaski* (New York: Van Nostrand, 1862), 14.

51. Schiller, *Sumter Is Avenged*, 137.

52. Cullum, *Biographical Register*, 2:367.

53. General Pemberton's view of abandoning the harbor forts and fighting the Union in the streets of Charleston disturbed local leaders and contributed to his reassignment.

54. Roswell Ripley, report, in *Year Book–1885, City of Charleston, South Carolina* (Charleston, SC: News and Courier Book Presses, 1885), 353.

55. Clement A. Evans, ed., *Confederate Military History*, Vol. 5 (Atlanta: Confederate Publishing Company, 1899): 99.

56. Roswell Ripley to William Herron Taylor, February 16, 1862, in *ORA*, Series 1, Vol. 6, 387.

57. John Johnson, *The Defense of Charleston Harbor Including Fort Sumter and the Adjacent Islands* (Charleston, SC: Walker, Evans and Cogswell, 1890), 22, 31.

58. Francis D. Lee, report, December 4, 1861, in *ORA*, Series 1, Vol. 6, 18–20; John A. Wagener, report on the bombardment of Fort Walker, November 11, 1861, in *ORA*, Series 1, Vol. 6, 14. In his post-action report, Lee lamented the offensive power of the fort and praised its defensive ability in protecting the garrison during the four-and-a-half-hour bombardment. Colonel John Wagener was critical of Francis Lee's design in that the navy was able to position ships to fire along the length of his channel batteries and disable it cannons. He repeated this flaw in the design he created for General Pemberton on Morris Island.

59. The engineering department personnel reflected the structure of the Confederate army in being composed of permanent or Confederate

States of America engineers, PCSA or temporary engineers, state militia engineers and civilian employees or volunteers.

60. Langdon was the oldest son of Langdon Cheves, former Speaker of the U.S. House of Representatives and president of the Bank of the United States.

61. Francis Gualdo Ravenel to Roswell Ripley, May 13, 1862, in *ORN*, Series 1, Vol. 12: 825–26.

62. John B. Marchand, Report, April 18, 1863, in *ORN*, Series 1, Vol. 12: 784–85.

63. Samuel F. Du Pont to Gideon Welles, August 19, 1862, in *ORN*, Series 1, Vol. 12, 825; Enoch Greenleaf Parrott to Samuel F. Du Pont, May 13, 1862, in *ORN*, Series 1, Vol. 12, 821.

64. Johnson, *Defense of Charleston Harbor*, app. clxviii.

65. John B. Marchand to Samuel F. Du Pont, May 29, 1862, in *ORN*, Series 1, Vol. 13 (Washington, D.C.: Government Printing Office, 1901), 53.

66. John Chatfield, report, July 12, 1862, in *ORA*, Series 1, Vol. 14, 36–37.

67. Joseph Holt, "Report upon the James Island Affair, June 16, 1862 by Colonel Joseph Holt," *Washington Chronicle*, February 20, 1864.

68. Patrick Brennan, *Secessionville* (Campbell, CA: Savas Publishing, 1996), 296–97.

69. Gustave T. Beauregard, "The Defense of Charleston," *North American Review* 356 (1886): 45–46.

70. C. Russell Horres Jr., "An Affair of Honor at Fort Sumter," *South Carolina Historical Magazine* 102, no. 1 (January 2001): 6–26.

Chapter 3

71. James M. McPherson, *Tried by War: Abraham Lincoln as Commander in Chief* (Toronto: Penguin Press HC, 2008).

72. Gustave T. Beauregard to William Henry C. Whiting, December 16, 1862, in *ORA*, Series 1, Vol. 14, 719.

73. Roman, *Military Operations*, 1:411.

74. Edward Palfrey, special orders 202, August 29, 1862, in *ORA*, Series 1, Vol. 14, 601; John C. Pemberton to Samuel Cooper, August 31, 1862, in *ORA*, Series 1, Vol. 14, 601.

75. Abraham Lincoln to Horace Greeley, *New York Tribune*, August 22, 1862.

76. Catharinus Putnam Buckingham to Edward Salomon, August 6, 1863, in *ORA*, Series 3, Vol. 2 (Washington, D.C.: 1899), 314.

77. Roger Ransom and Richard Sutch, "Capitalists without Capital: The Burden of Slavery and the Impact of Emancipation," *Agricultural History* 62, no. 3 (1988): 133–60.

78. Gene Dattel, *Cotton and Race in the Making of America* (Lanham, MD: Ivan R. Dee, 2011), 36.

79. Abraham Lincoln, January 1, 1863, in *ORA*, Series 3, Vol. 3 (Washington, D.C.: Government Printing Office), 3.

80. Rufus Saxton to Edward Stanton, January 25, 1863, in *ORA*, Series 3, Vol. 3, 20.

81. John Speer, *The Life of James Henry Lane* (Garden City, KS: John Speer Printer, 1896), 262.

82. Richard G. Ward to Colonel J.M. Williams, October 29, 1862, in *ORA*, Series 1, Vol. 53, 455.

83. Edwin Stanton to John A. Andrews, January 26, 1863, in *ORA*, Series 3, Vol. 3, 20–21.

84. Levi C. Turner to Edwin Stanton, September 30, 1862, in *ORA*, Series 2, Vol. 4 (Washington, D.C.: Government Printing Office, 1899), 585.

85. Hugh W. Mercer to Thomas Jordan, November 14, 1862, in *ORA*, Series 2, Vol. 4, 945.

86. Jefferson Davis, General Orders 11, December 24, 1862, in *ORA*, Series 2, Vol. 5 (Washington, D.C.: Government Printing Office, 1899), 795–97.

87. James M. Matthew, ed., *Statues at Large of the Confederate States of America* (Richmond: H.M. Smith Printer, 1863), 168.

88. Joseph Brevard, A.A. 1740, P.L. 167, *An Alphabetical Digest of the Public Statute Law of South-Carolina*, 2:233.

89. Daniel Horsmanden, *The New York Conspiracy* (New York: Southwick & Pelsue, 1810).

90. Charleston City Council, *An Account of the Late Intended Insurrection among a Portion of the Blacks of the City of Charleston, South Carolina* (Boston: Joseph W. Ingraham, 1822).

91. Frederick Douglass, *Life and Times of Frederick Douglass* (Hartford: Park Publishing, 1882), 387.

Chapter 4

92. Charles J. Villere, *Review of Certain Remarks of the President When Requested to Restore General Beauregard to the Command of Department No. 2* (Charleston, SC: Evans and Coggswell, 1863). For a detailed examination of the difficulties

between Davis and Beauregard see Yves Réné LeMonnier, "General Beauregard at Shiloh, April 6, 1862," *Neale's Monthly* 3 (January 1914): 146–65.

93. Gustave T. Beauregard to Charles H. Villere, September 2, 1862, in *ORA*, Series 1, Vol. 52, Part 2 (Washington, D.C.: Government Printing Office, 1898), 344. Governor Pickens had expressed dissatisfaction with General John C. Pemberton, which gave Davis the opportunity to reassign Pemberton to head of the Department of Mississippi and West Louisiana and place Beauregard in the post, which amounted to a demotion. Beauregard wrote Congressman Charles Villere, "I am tired of forming armies for others to fight, I prefer Charleston."

94. Horres, "An Affair of Honor at Fort Sumter," 6–26.

95. George G. Kundahl, Chapter 8 in *Confederate Engineer: Training and Campaigning with John Morris Wampler* (Knoxville: University of Tennessee Press, 2000). Captain John M. Wampler was killed at Battery Wagner on August 17, 1863, just ten days after joining Beauregard's engineering staff. His sword is in the Charleston Museum.

96. Roman, *Military Operations*, 2:276–77. A West Point graduate and native of Goochland, Virginia, Harris had been with Beauregard as a staff engineer since before the Battle of First Manassas and constructed a number of fortifications along the Mississippi prior to his tenure at Charleston. Beauregard later recommended promoting Harris to brigadier general with command of the Charleston District, but before learning of his promotion and assuming command, Harris died in Summerville, South Carolina, on October 10, 1864, of yellow fever.

97. Bernard H. Nelson, "Confederate Slave Impressment Legislation, 1861–1865," *Journal of Negro History* 31, no. 4 (October 1946): 392–410. Although enlisting slaves in the Confederate army was resisted during the war, tens of thousands of slaves were impressed by the Confederate and state governments to build and maintain roads, bridges, railroads and fortifications. The workmen referred to in the official records are most likely impressed slaves, although some free persons of color and white laborers were hired by the engineers.

98. John C. Pemberton, summary of guns bearing on Charleston Harbor on September 22, in *ORA*, Series 1, Vol. 14, 606.

99. Beauregard, "The Defense of Charleston," 421.

100. Tabular statement of the works in the Department of South Carolina, October 4, 1862, in *ORA*, Series 1, Vol. 14, 627; Roswell S. Ripley to Thomas Jordan, October 25, 1862, in *ORA*, Series 1, Vol. 14, 653–654.

In the October 4 report, it is referred to as the Morris Island battery and is listed as complete with its eleven guns. Ripley's letter of the same month reports five guns mounted, two awaiting carriages and a garrison of two companies of artillery and one regiment of infantry.

101. Beauregard, "The Defense of Charleston," 429. Beauregard emphatically states that neither Pemberton nor Ripley were skilled in military engineering.

102. Roman, *Military Operations*, 2:11–13. In his recapitulation of the Charleston harbor defenses on September 29, 1862, no mention of works on Morris Island possibly reflects Beauregard's concern for the inadequacy of the work.

103. Roswell S. Ripley, increase of forces, October 25, 1862, in *ORA*, Series 1, Vol. 14, 655.

104. David B. Harris to Thomas Jordan, June 11, 1863, in *ORA*, Series 1, Vol.14, 971; Quincy A. Gillmore to S. Du Pont, June 26, 1863, in *ORN*, Series 1, Vol. 1 (Washington, D.C.: Government Printing Office), 299. The name "Battery Wagner" was typically used by the Confederates during and after the war and probably reflected its humble beginnings rather than its size and capability. Some, such as chief engineer David Harris, used the terms "fort" and "battery" interchangeably. The Union initially referenced it as Battery Wagner and then more generally as Fort Wagner.

105. Charles H. Olmstead, *Reminiscences of Service with the First Volunteers of Georgia, Charleston Harbor, in 1863: An Address Delivered before the Georgia Historical Society, March 3, 1879* (Savannah: J.H. Estill, 1879), 10. The powder magazine, located under the seafront bastion, appears to have been part of the original design, as it differs significantly in alignment from the other magazines. Magazines had entrances directed away from the expected angle of fire and designed with right angles to prevent exploding shell fragments from entering. This made the interiors dark and required protected air shafts to ventilate moisture. For safety, interior lighting was provided by specially designed magazine lanterns. Olmstead reported that on July 24, 1863, an enemy shell struck an air flue and exploded. The flash of light entered the magazine to the terror of men working inside.

106. Gustave T. Beauregard to S. Cooper, September 30, 1863, in *ORA*, Series 1, Vol. 28, Part 1, 92.

107. Gustave T. Beauregard to Roswell S. Ripley, February 8, 1863, in *ORA*, Series 1, Vol. 14: 769–70. Beauregard called for an open three-gun battery on Cummings Point, later to be called Battery Gregg after Confederate

general Maxcy Gregg, who died at Fredericksburg in December 1862.

108. Roman, *Military Operations*, 2:105–6. Beauregard had about thirty thousand effective troops to cover all of South Carolina and Georgia in April 1863. By July, this had been reduced to about fifteen thousand.

Chapter 5

109. Douglas E. Campbell and Stephen Chant, *Patent Log: Innovative Patents that Advanced the US Navy* (Washington, D.C.: Syneca Research, 2013), 242; John M. Brooke, June 23, 1861 journal entry, in *Ironclads and Big Guns of the Confederacy*, ed. George M. Brooke Jr. (Columbia: University of South Carolina Press, 2002), 22.

110. John M. Brooke, September 2, 1861 journal entry, in *Ironclads and Big Guns*, 37.

111. John M. Brooke, October 4, 1861 journal entry, in *Ironclads and Big Guns*, 43.

112. John M. Brooke, November 2, 1861 journal entry, in *Ironclads and Big Guns*, 44, 48.

113. *Hearings Before the U.S. House Committee on Naval Affairs*, Sixty-Second Cong. 1625–37 (1911) (statement of Theodore Ruggles Timby).

114. *Journal of the House of Representatives* 37, issue 2 (1862): 308.

115. William H. Roberts, *Civil War Ironclads: The U.S. Navy and Industrial Mobilization* (Baltimore: Johns Hopkins University Press, 2000), 5. While the South struggled to build a handful of ironclad rams, the North's superior industrial capacity built fifty of them in under two years.

116. Stephen Mallory to William Webb, February 19, 1863, in *ORN*, Series 1, Vol. 13, 821.

117. Thomas F. Drayton, report 2, March 23, 1862, in *ORA*, Series 1, Vol. 6, 104; William R. Boggs, *The Military Reminiscences of Gen. Wm. R. Boggs, C.S.A.*, The John Lawson Monographs of the Trinity College Historical Society 3 (Durham, NC: Seeman Printery, 1913), 24.

118. Oswald Garrison Villard, "Submarine and Torpedo in the Blockade of the Confederacy," *Harper's Monthly Magazine* 133 (1916): 133.

119. John S. Barnes, *Submarine Warfare, Offensive and Defensive, Including a Discussion of the Offensive Torpedo System, Its Effects upon Iron-Clad Ship Systems, and Influence upon Future Naval Wars* (New York: Van Nostrand, 1869), 66.

120. Gustave T. Beauregard to Samuel Cooper, October 3, 1862, in *ORA*, Series 1, Vol. 14, 619.

121. Gustave T. Beauregard, enclosure A, September 29, 1862, in *ORA*, Series 1, Vol. 14, 621–22.

122. William A. Webb, report, October 19, 1864, in *ORN*, Series 1, Vol. 14 (Washington, D.C.: Government Printing Office, 1902), 290–92.

123. Regimental strength varied in the Civil War depending on attrition and recruitment. Authorized at ten one-hundred-man companies, regiments typically mustered half to three-quarters of that.

124. Jacob Newton Cardozo, *Reminiscences of Charleston* (Charleston, SC: Joseph Walker Printer, 1866), 97.

125. Beauregard, "Torpedo Service in the Harbor," 160.

126. Roswell Ripley, report, April 13, 1863, in *ORA*, Series 1, Vol. 14, 263.

127. Cleland Kinloch Huger, report, April 8, 1863, in *ORA*, Series 1, Vol. 14, 276.

128. Charles G. de Lisle to G.T. Beauregard, May 25, 1863, in *ORA*, Series 1, Vol. 14, 948–52.

129. Major William H. Echols, Report, April 9, 1863, in *ORA*, Series 1, Vol. 14, 249. Other than the three men killed by an exploding magazine chest at Battery Wagner, the only other Confederate death was a soldier killed at Fort Moultrie by a falling flagpole.

130. "The Fight in Charleston from the *Charleston Mercury*," *New York Times*, April 26, 1863.

131. Johnson, *Defense of Charleston Harbor*, 71.

132. Samuel F. Du Pont, report no. 208, April 22, 1863, in *ORN*, Series 1. Vol. 14: 51–56.

133. David Hunter to H.W. Halleck, April 15, 1863, in *ORA*, Series 1, Vol. 14, 442.

134. Cullum, *Biographical Register*, 1:607.

135. Thomas Seymour to Israel Vodges, April 22, 1863, in *ORA*, Series 1, Vol. 14, 446.

Chapter 6

136. Abraham Lincoln to General Hunter and Admiral DuPont, April 14, 1863, in *ORA*, Series 1, Vol. 14, 441.

137. David Hunter to H.W. Halleck, May 11, 1863, in *ORA*, Series 1, Vol. 14, 453–54.

138. Rowena Weed, *Combined Operations of the Civil War* (Lincoln: University of Nebraska Press, 1993), 298.

139. Horace Greeley to John G. Nicolay, May 21, 1863, Lincoln Papers, Library of Congress.

140. Quincy A. Gillmore to George Cullum, May 23, 1863, in *ORA*, Series 1, Vol. 14, 459.

141. Quincy A. Gillmore to Henry W. Halleck, June 5, 1863, in *ORA*, Series 1, Vol. 14, 465.

142. John Cunningham Kelton, special orders 259, June 3, 1863, in *ORA*, Series 1, Vol. 14, 464.

143. David Hunter to H.W. Halleck, May 11, 1863, in *ORA*, Series 1, Vol. 14, 453–54; David Hunter to Abraham Lincoln, June 25, 1963, in *ORA*, Series 1, Vol. 14, 469. Hunter, a friend of Lincoln, was at a loss as to why Lincoln replaced him. Hunter had proposed an identical plan of operations at Charleston after the ironclad attack.

144. James Mason Hoppins, *The Life of Andrew Hull Foote* (New York: Harper Brothers, 1874), 378.

145. Gideon Welles to John A. Dahlgren, June 24, 1863, in *ORN*, Series 1, Vol. 14, 295. Dahlgren, arriving late to the operation, never felt comfortable with a supporting role and developed a lifelong enmity with Quincy Gillmore; see Madeline Vinton Dahlgren, *Memoir of John A. Dahlgren, Rear-Admiral United States Navy* (Boston: James R. Osgood Co., 1882).

146. Milledge L. Bonham to Gustave T. Beauregard, April 24, 1863, in *ORA*, Series 1, Vol. 14, 911.

147. Gustave T. Beauregard to James H. Trapier, April 5, 1863, in *ORA*, Series 1, Vol. 14, 881.

148. Roswell S. Ripley to Thomas Jordan, May 24, 1863, in *ORA*, Series 1, Vol. 14, app. 1021.

149. Langdon Cheves to David B. Harris, June 9, 1863, in *ORA*, Series 1, Vol. 14, 958.

150. Battery Wagner was a work in progress from its inception through its occupation. Post-occupation drawings do not give an accurate reflection of its design and artillery placements during earlier events. Union engineers also made significant modifications to its armament after they occupied the works. Daily reports of the commanding officers of the battery clearly show that changes to the structure and armament were evolving right up to the end of the siege and beyond in response to military necessity.

151. Roswell S. Ripley to Thomas Jordan, June 14, 1863, in *ORA*, Series 1, Vol. 28, Part 2, 140.

152. Beauregard, "The Defense of Charleston," 424. Beauregard describes this activity as almost entirely rebuilding the battery.

153. Robert Cogdell Gilchrist, *Confederate Defense of Morris Island* (Charleston, SC: News and Courier Book Presses, 1889), 8–9.

154. Olmstead, *Reminiscences of Service*, 5.

155. Hansford Dade Duncan Twiggs, "The Defense of Battery Wagner," *Addresses Delivered before the Confederate Veterans Association* (Savannah: G.N. Nichols, 1898), 76.

Chapter 7

156. Departmental returns, July 1863, in *ORA*, Series 1, Vol. 28, Part 2, 31. In the Civil War, regiments were commanded by a colonel. Three to four regiments were combined under a general into brigades, several brigades were combined into a division, and several divisions were combined into a corps. Q.A. Gillmore was a corps commander.

157. Abstract from returns, July 1863, in *ORA*, Series 1, Vol. 28, Part 2, 31.

158. Joseph A. Yates, report, November 27, 1863, in *ORA*, Series 1, Vol. 28, Part 1, 529.

159. George C. Strong, report, July 10, 1863, in *ORA*, Series 1, Vol. 28, Part 1, 354.

160. Cardozo, *Reminiscences of Charleston*, 99.

161. Joseph A. Yates, report, July 17, 1863, in *ORA*, Series 1, Vol. 28, Part 1: 527.

162. Eldridge Copp, *Reminiscences of the War of Rebellion 1861–1865* (Nashua, NH: Telegraph Publishing Company, 1911), 238.

163. John A. Dahlgren, report, July 13, 1863, in *ORN*, Series 1, Vol. 14, 320.

164. Roman, *Military Operations*, 2:114.

165. Stephen R. Wise, *Gate of Hell: Campaign for Charleston Harbor 1863* (Columbia: University of South Carolina Press, 1994), 76.

166. J.A. Dahlgren, report, July 13, 1863, in *ORN*, Series 1, Vol. 14, 321. Admiral Dahlgren was at a serious disadvantage in the opening days of the campaign for Morris Island. He arrived off Charleston on Monday, July 6, and was in action on July 10. General Gillmore was well advanced in his plans and obviously did not inform Dahlgren of all the particulars.

167. M. Martin Gray, report, August 12, 1863, in *ORA*, Series 1, Vol. 28, Part 1, 523.

Chapter 8

168. Moving heavy Parrott rifles required hundreds of men to unload them from barges onto the beach at Lighthouse Inlet and then drag them hanging under large wheeled carts down the beach and across the soft sand to positions prepared for them. To hoist them into position, a tripod arrangement with block and tackle was employed. Most of this work was accomplished under the cover of darkness to avoid attracting Confederate artillery fire.
169. Quincy A. Gillmore, report, November 1863, in *ORA*, Series 1, Vol. 28, Part 1, 8.
170. With Union batteries within range of Battery Wagner, communication via Vincent's Creek was not practical. Supplies and reinforcements were brought in from Cummings Point.
171. Thomas B. Brooks, journal, September 27, 1863, in *ORA*, Series 1, Vol. 28, Part 1, 271.
172. Henry F.W. Little, *The Seventh Regiment New Hampshire Volunteers in the War of the Rebellion* (Concord, NH: Ira C. Evans, 1896), 113. Fort Sumter mounted two seven-inch Brooke rifles that could fire shells the entire length of Morris Island.
173. Abstract from returns, July 1863, in *ORA*, Series 1, Vol. 28, Part 2, 31.
174. John A. Dahlgren to Gideon Welles, July 18, 1863, in *ORN*, Series 1, Vol. 14, 358; John A. Dahlgren, diary entry, July 18, 1863, in *ORN*, Series 1, Vol. 14, 366.
175. Gilchrist, *Confederate Defense of Morris Island*, 18.
176. Mallet, John William, "Work of the Ordnance Bureau of the War Department of the Confederate States, 1861–5," *Southern Historical Society Papers* 37 (1909): 9.
177. Twiggs, "The Defense of Battery Wagner," 79, 83.
178. Stephen Walkey, *History of the 7th Connecticut Volunteer Infantry, Hawley's Brigade, Terry's Division, Tenth Army Corps, 1861–1865* (Hartford, CT, 1905), 81.
179. Abraham J. Palmer, *The History of the 48th Regiment of New York* (Brooklyn: Veterans Association of the Regiment, 1885), 101.
180. Roswell S. Ripley to General Thomas Jordan, July 22, 1863, in *ORA*, Series 1, Vol. 28, Part 1, 372.
181. William W.H. Davis, report, July 31, 1863, in *ORA*, Series 1, Vol. 1, 583–85.

182. Edward L. Pierce to Mr. and Mrs. Shaw, July 22, 1863, *Memorial to Robert Gould Shaw* (Cambridge, MA: University Press, 1864), 54–55; Private letters, in *The Third New Hampshire and All about It*, ed. Daniel Eldredge (Boston: E.B. Stillings Co., 1881), 324. Edward Pierce, in writing to Shaw's parents about his death in the assault, mentioned that Shaw had developed a friendship with General George C. Strong, a fellow Massachusetts native, in the brief time the Fifty-Fourth was at St. Helena Island. In 1881, General Gillmore was specifically asked why the Fifty-Fourth had been assigned to the lead. He replied that he had no knowledge of the assignments, which had been delegated to General Seymour. Seymour, in response to the same question, replied in 1881 that to his knowledge, Shaw was not consulted in the matter and that the Fifty-Fourth was one of the strongest and best-officered regiments.

183. Truman Seymour, report, November 10, 1863, in *ORA*, Series 1, Vol. 28, Part 1, 347.

184. Muzzle-loading rifles commonly employed a small metal cap containing an impact-sensitive compound to fire the black powder charge when struck by a spring-loaded hammer actuated by pulling the trigger.

185. Luis Fenellosa Emilio, *A Brave Black Regiment: The History of the 54th Massachusetts Volunteer Infantry, 1863–1865* (Boston: Boston Book Company, 1894), 75, 79.

186. E.K. Bryan, correspondence to the *Fayetteville Observer*, August 3, 1863 (transcribed by Christine Spencer, February 2008). In his letter, the adjutant reported that two companies of the Thirty-First North Carolina were at Battery Gregg and eight at Battery Wagner. The regimental strength was only 380 effectives. This indicates that about 300 men were at Wagner. The unit suffered 36 casualties during the bombardment and battle.

187. Warren Adams, report, July 21, 1863, in *ORA*, Series 1, Vol. 28, Part 1, 535–36.

188. David L. Crawley, report, July 22, 1863, in *ORA*, Series 1, Vol. 28, Part 1, 570.

189. Quincy A. Gillmore, report of operations, November 15, 1863, in *ORA*, Series 1, Vol. 28, Part 1, 16.

190. Emilio, *Brave Black Regiment*, 80.

191. Lewis Butler, report, February 2, 1864, in *ORA*, Series 1, Vol. 53, 6.

192. Franklin E. Town, report, September 11, 1863, in *ORA*, Series 1, Vol. 28, Part 1, 47.

193. George B. Dandy, report, November 4, 1863, in *ORA*, Series 1, Vol. 53, 11.
194. Palmer, *History of the 48th Regiment*, 103; Hector McKethan, report, July 20, 1863, in *ORA*, Series 1, Vol. 28, Part 1, 525; Roswell S. Ripley to Thomas Jordan, July 18, 1863, in *ORA*, Series 1, Vol. 28, Part 1, 369. Abraham Palmer, a participant in the attack, described it as three separate assaults: the Fifty-Fourth, the balance of the First Brigade and then the Second Brigade. Three separate assaults were also reported by Colonel McKethan defending the curtain and by General Ripley.
195. Special orders no. 251, July 18, 1863, in *ORA*, Series 1, Vol. 28, Part 2, 209.
196. Abraham J. Palmer, "Rebel Prisons: Mr. Palmer's Thrilling Account of the Capture of Fort Wagner," *New York Times*, March 21, 1882.
197. Account of Henry G. Webber, in Eldredge, *The Third New Hampshire*, 321; Copp, *Reminiscences of the War*, 247. When Putnam deployed his brigade by a column of regiments, only six of the ten companies could pass between the marsh and the beach in front of Battery Wagner.
198. Gabriel James Rains to James A. Seddon, August 31, 1863, in *ORA*, Series 1, Vol. 28, Part 2, 324. There are a number of accounts reporting the use of hand grenades by the Confederate defenders. The chief of the arsenal at Augusta, Brigadier General G.J. Rains, said that there were no hand grenades at Battery Wagner but "subterra shells" (land mines).
199. Roswell S. Ripley, report, July 22, 1863, in *ORA*, Series 1, Vol. 28, Part 1, 371. See also William L. De Pass, report, July 19, 1863, in *ORA*, Series 1, Vol. 28, Part 1, 549.
200. M. Martin Gray, report no. 35, August 12, 1863, in *ORA*, Series 1, Vol. 28, Part 1, 523.
201. Gustave T. Beauregard to Joseph E. Johnston, July 19, 1863, in *ORA*, Series 1, Vol. 28, Part 2, 210.

Chapter 9

202. Gilchrist, *Confederate Defense of Morris Island*, 26; Paul Hamilton Hayne, "The Defense of Battery Wagner," *The Southern Bivouac*, eds. William Naylor McDonald, Basil W. Duke and Richard W. Knott (Louisville: B.F. Avery and Sons, 1886), 1:606.
203. Gustave T. Beauregard to James A. Seddon, July 20, 1863, in *ORA*, Series 1, Vol. 28, Part 1, 58.

204. Lawrence Massillon Keitt to Gustave T. Beauregard, September 6, 1863, in *ORA*, Series 1, Vol. 25, Part 1 (Washington, D.C.: Government Printing Office, 1889), 89.

205. Henry Wager Halleck to Quincy A. Gillmore, July 28, 1863, in *ORA*, Series 1, Vol. 28, Part 2, 29–30.

206. Later that fall, General Gillmore had medals cast to be given out by the various units involved in the Morris Island campaign on which he memorialized the date, August 23, 1863.

207. The two-hundred-pound Parrott rifle, firing at extreme elevation and with maximum charges, failed after thirty-two rounds. It was recovered as a war souvenir and sits today in Cadwalader Park in Trenton, New Jersey.

208. Quincy A. Gillmore to Alfred H. Terry, August 2, 1863, in *ORA*, Series 1, Vol. 23, Part 2 (Washington, D.C.: Government Printing Office), 35.

209. James H. Gooding, correspondence to the *New Bedford Mercury*, September 15, 1863, in *On the Alter of Freedom*, ed. Virginia M. Adams (New York: Warner Books, 1992), 54.

210. Dodge, David, "Free Negroes of North Carolina," *Atlantic Monthly* 57, no. 339 (1886): 20–30.

211. Thomas B. Brooks, note 18, "Working Parties and Health of Troop," in *ORA*, Series 1, Vol. 28, Part 1, 326–28.

212. Thomas B. Brooks, note 19 and addenda, "Colored Troops for Work," in *ORA*, Ser. 1, Vol. 28, Part 1, 328–31.

213. Quincy A. Gillmore, report of operations, November 15, 1863, in *ORA*, Series 1, Vol. 28, Part 1, 26.

214. Gustave T. Beauregard, report of operations, September 18, 1864, in *ORA*, Series 1, Vol. 28, Part 1, 27, 91.

215. Peter S. Michie, report, February 1, 1864, in *ORA*, Series 1, Vol. 28, Part 1, 339–40.

216. Charles Cotesworth Pinckney, report no. 33, September 8, 1863, in *ORA*, Series 1, Vol. 28, Part 1, 520–21.

217. Returns of casualties, in ORA, Series 1, Vol. 28, Part 1, 407–9.

218. Ibid., 210.

219. Thomas Benton Brooks, report, September 27, 1863, in *ORA*, Series 1, Vol. 28, Part 1, 237.

220. William Furness, "The Siege of Fort Wagner," *Military Essays and Recollections: Papers Read before the Commandery of the State of Illinois, Military Order of the Loyal Legion of the United States* (Chicago: A.C. McClurg and Company, 1891), 229.

221. Frederic Denison, *Shot and Shell: The Third Rhode Island Heavy Artillery Regiment in the Rebellion* (Providence: J.A. Reid, 1879), 266.

222. *The Sanitary Commission of the United States Army: A Succinct Narrative of Its Works and Purpose* (New York: Published for the Benefit of the United States Sanitary Commission, 1864), 277.

223. Thomas Jordan to Roswell Ripley, July 17, 1863, in *ORA*, Series 1, Vol. 28, Part 2, 206.

Chapter 10

224. The so-called limelights required a source of oxygen and hydrogen, which was prepared on Morris Island by a team of thirty-two soldiers and workmen often working under Confederate artillery fire. Robert Grant, "Improvements in Lime Light," *Journal of the Franklin Institute*, Series 3, Vol. 52 (1866): 280.

225. For an excellent analysis of how Gillmore's success at Fort Pulaski led to his strategic failure in descending on Morris Island, see Adam J. Lewis, *The Civil War Experiences of General Quincy Adams Gillmore: The Challenges of Transitioning from the Tactical to the Operational Level of Command*, US Army School of Advanced Military Studies Monographs (Fort Leavenworth, KS: School of Advanced Military Studies, 2011).

226. John G. Foster to Henry W. Halleck, July 7, 1864, in *ORA*, Series 1, Vol. 35, Part 1, 15.

227. John G. Foster to Henry W. Halleck, July 12, 1864, in *ORA*, Series 1, Vol. 35, Part 1, 18.

228. Thomas Jordan to David B. Harris, July 23, 1863, in *ORA*, Series 1, Vol. 28, Part 2, 221.

229. Arthur M. Wilcox and Warren Ripley, *The Civil War at Charleston* (Charleston, SC: Charleston Evening Post, 1966). Arthur Wilcox and Warren Ripley identified over sixty fortified positions guarding the Charleston area.

230. John A. Dahlgren to Quincy A. Gillmore, September 8, 1863, in *ORA*, Series 1, Vol. 28, Part 2, 87.

231. Quincy A. Gillmore to John Dahlgren, September 8, 1863, in *ORA*, Series 1, Vol. 28, Part 2, 88.

232. Stephen Elliott, report no. 2, September 9, 1863, in *ORA*, Series 1, Vol. 28, Part 1, 725–27.

233. Samuel F. Du Pont to Gideon Welles, April 11, 1864, in *ORN*, Series 1, Vol. 14, 242.

234. John A. Dahlgren, report of January 16, 1865, in *ORN*, Series 1 , Vol. 16 (Washington, D.C.: Government Printing Office, 1906), 171–75.

235. Madeline Vinton Dahlgren, February 5, 1865 entry, in *Memoir of John A. Dahlgren, Rear-Admiral United States Navy* (Boston: J.R. Osgood and Company, 1882), 494.

236. John A. Dahlgren, report regarding operations against the defenses of Charleston, October 16, 1865, in *ORN*, Series 1, Vol. 16, 429–55.

237. Percival Drayton to Lydig M. Hoyt, February 28, 1863, in "Naval Letters of Percival Drayton 1861–1865," *New York Public Library Bulletin No. 10* (1909): 615; Dahlgren, report regarding operations, 437.

238. Quincy A. Gillmore, "The Army before Charleston in 1863," in *Battles and Leaders of the Civil War*, eds. Robert Underwood Johnson and Clarence Clough Buel (New York: Century Company, 1888), 4:52–71.

239. Furness, "The Siege of Fort Wagner," 226.

240. Roswell S. Ripley, *Correspondence Relating to the Fortification of Morris Island and Operations of Engineers, Charleston, S.C. 1863* (New York: John J. Caulon Printing, 1878); Beauregard, "The Defense of Charleston," 429. When Ripley's associates tried to give Ripley credit for Charleston's defense, Beauregard rebutted, saying that Ripley had no knowledge of military engineering.

241. Roman, *Military Operations*, 2:143.

242. John E. Florance Jr., "Morris Island: Victory or Blunder?," *South Carolina Historical and Genealogical Magazine* 55, no. 3, (July 1954): 152. In his analysis of Gillmore's operation, John Florance of the U.S. Navy described it as a failure.

243. Quincy A. Gillmore to Henry W. Halleck, September 24, 1863, in *ORA*, Series 1, Vol. 28, Part 2, 96.

244. John Rodgers, February 4, 1864 testimony, in Dahlgren, report regarding operations, 440.

245. Roman, *Military Operations*, 2:135.

246. Quincy A. Gillmore to H.W. Halleck, February 26, 1865, in *ORA*, Series 1, Vol. 47, Part 1 (Washington, D.C.: Government Printing Office, 1895), 1008.

247. Following the war, a sand model of the battery was created and used for teaching siege tactics at the U.S. Military Academy until World War I rewrote the book on trench warfare.

248. Justus Schiebert, *A Prussian Observes the American Civil War—The Military Studies of Justus Schiebert*, ed. Frederic Trautman (Columbia: University of Missouri Press, 2001), 91.
249. William Watts Hart Davis to Adrian Terry, February 4, 1864, in *ORA*, Series 1, Vol. 35, Part 1, 467.
250. John Ogden Murray, *The Immortal Six Hundred* (Roanoke, VA: Stone Printing, 1911).
251. Thomas C. Jervey, "Charleston during the Civil War," in *Annual Report of the American Historical Association for the Year 1913* (Washington, D.C.: American Historical Association, 1915), 1:172–73.
252. Emilio, *Brave Black Regiment*, 201.
253. Beauregard, "Defense of Charleston," 46.
254. Joseph K. Barnes, *Medical and Surgical History of the War of the Rebellion* (Washington, D.C.: Government Printing Office, 1870), Part 1, 343–47.
255. Quincy Gillmore, abstracts of returns of the Department of the South for January 1864, in *ORA*, Series 1, Vol. 35, Part 1, 463.
256. Wise, *Gate of Hell*, 241.
257. Johnson, *Defense of Charleston Harbor*, 273.
258. Ibid., 266.
259. Soldiers' Directory of Public Offices, *Charleston Courier*, January 6, 1864, 2.
260. Roman, *Military Operations*, 2:277.
261. Patrick R. Cleburne, et al., memorandum to the commanders of the Army of Tennessee regarding the freeing and arming of slaves, January 2, 1864, in *ORA*, Series 1, Vol. 52, Part 2, 587.
262. In particular, General George McClellan and Major General John A. McClernand asked Lincoln to rescind the proclamation. General John G. Foster was adamantly opposed to the concept of black troops. Jefferson C. Davis, another veteran of Fort Sumter, abandoned hundreds of freed slaves at Ebenezer Creek on Sherman's march to the sea.
263. *Memorial to Robert Gould Shaw*, 105.
264. Emilio, *Brave Black Regiment*, 97, 101. Federal authorities reported 106 men missing after the assault. Of those, 60 are reported to have been captured. Twenty of the captured were wounded. At end of the war, 27 survived confinement in the Charleston Jail and the Florence Stockade.
265. Iredell Jones to his father, July 20, 1863, "Letters from Fort Sumter," in *Southern Historical Society Papers January to December, 1884* (Richmond: Wm. Ellis Jones, Printer, 1884), 138.

266. Denison, *Shot and Shell*, 173.
267. "The employment of colored men as soldiers, usually regarded at the formation of these regiments as a mere experiment, has now become of universal acception." (Governor John A. Andrew to the Massachusetts Legislature, November 1863).
268. Edwin M. Stanton to Abraham Lincoln, December 5, 1863, in *ORA*, Series 3, Vol. 3, 1132.
269. J. Holt to E.M. Stanton, August 20, 1863, in *ORA*, Series 3, Vol. 3, 696. A month after the assault of the Fifty-Fourth Massachusetts at Battery Wagner, the judge advocate wrote the secretary of war that the president was fully convinced of the capabilities of the African American soldier and urged the employment of "a most powerful and reliable arm of public defense."
270. Abraham Lincoln to James Wadsworth, ca. January 1864, in *The Collected Works of Abraham Lincoln*, ed. Roy P. Basler (New Brunswick, NJ: Rutgers University Press, 1953), 7:101–2. Although President Lincoln did not live to see the African American male receive the right to vote, he avowed that African American soldiers had earned the right with their blood. Lincoln recommended that black troops be protected from Southern retaliation, and many units were reserved for garrison duty. This did not prevent three African Americans from earning the Medal of Honor in fighting in South Carolina: Robert Blake, William H. Carney and Andrew Jackson Smith.
271. Editorial, *New York Daily Tribune*, September 5, 1865, 4.

Chapter 11

272. Emilio, *Brave Black Regiment*, 107.
273. Ibid., 179.
274. Ibid., 227, 230.
275. Ibid., 366, 386.
276. Robert J. Zalimas Jr., "A Disturbance in the City," in *Black Soldiers in Blue: African American Soldiers in the Civil War* (Chapel Hill: University of North Carolina Press, 2001), 388.
277. Emilio, *Brave Black Regiment*, 330–31.
278. Ibid, 315.
279. Ibid., 169, 296.
280. Pieter Spierenburg, ed., "White Supremacist Justice and the Rule of Law: Lynching, Honor, and the State in Ben Tillman's South Carolina,"

Men and Violence: Masculinity, Honor Codes and Violent Rituals in Europe and America (Columbus: Ohio State University Press, 1998), 213–39.

281. Henry Lee Moon, "Negro Suffrage," *National Civic Review* 59, no. 5 (1970): 246.

282. Walter C. Hamm, "The Three Phases of Negro Suffrage," *The North American Review* 168 (1899): 292.

283. Samuel F. Du Pont to Gideon Welles, August 19, 1862, in *ORN*, Series 1, Vol. 12, 825.

284. W.H. Peronneau to W.F. Nance, July 19, 1863, in *ORA*, Series 2, Vol. 6 (Washington, D.C.: Government Printing Office, 1899), 132.

285. Gustave T. Beauregard to Sam Cooper, July 22, 1863, in *ORA*, Series 2, Vol. 6, 134.

286. James A. Seddon to Gustave T. Beauregard, July 22, 1863, in *ORA*, Series 2, Vol. 6, 139.

287. Milledge L. Bonham to Gustave T. Beauregard, July 22, 1863, in *ORA*, Series 2, Vol. 6, 139–40.

288. Milledge L. Bonham to James Seddon, July 23, 1863, in *ORA*, Series 2, Vol. 6, 145–46.

289. Thomas Jordan to Nathaniel Savage Crowell, July 23, 1863, in *ORA*, Series 2, Vol. 6, 146.

290. James A. Seddon to Milledge L. Bonham, August 1, 1863, in *ORA*, Series 2, Vol. 6, 169.

291. Milledge L. Bonham to James A. Seddon, August 10, 1863, in *ORA*, Series 2, Vol. 6, 193–94.

292. James A. Seddon to Milledge L. Bonham, September 1, 1863, in *ORA*, Series 2, Vol. 6, 245–46.

293. Milledge L. Bonham to James A. Seddon, August 23, 1863, in Emilio, *Brave Black Regiment*, 409.

294. Emilio, *Brave Black Regiment*, 423–24.

295. William H. Ludlow to Robert Ould, June 14, 1863, in *ORA*, Series 2, Vol. 6, 17–18.

296. Thomas Wentworth Higginson, *Army Life in a Black Regiment* (New York: Cambridge University Press, 1870), 292.

297. "Brave Sergeant Carney Dies of Accidental Injuries," *Boston Post*, December 10, 1908: 9.

298. Booker T. Washington, *Up From Slavery: An Autobiography* (Garden City, NJ: Doubleday & Company, 1901), 251.

299. Martin Blat, et al., eds., *Hope and Glory, Essays on the Legacy of the Fifty-Fourth Massachusetts Regiment* (Amherst: University of Massachusetts Press, 2009).

300. Ester Hill Hawks, *A Woman Doctor's Civil War: Ester Hill Hawks' Diary*, ed. Gerald Schwartz (Columbia: University of South Carolina Press, 1989), 90; National Medical Museum Collection, Silver Spring, MD.

301. Quincy A. Gillmore, report, November 15, 1863, in *ORA*, Series 1, Vol. 28, Part 1, 14.

302. Report of State Officers, Board and Committees to the General Assembly of South Carolina (1879), 862.

303. Quincy A. Gillmore, report of operations, "Report of the Chief of Engineers," in the *Annual Report of the Secretary of War* (Washington, D.C.: Government Printing Office, 1884), 2:1080.

304. Palmer, *History of the 48th Regiment*, 127.

305. *Charleston Courier*, May 10, 1884: 1. A visit to the island on May 9, 1884, by Robert C. Gilchrist, Charles E. Chichester and former Union engineer Thomas B. Brooks revealed that nothing was left of the battery or of the Union trench works.

INDEX

About the Author

Russell Horres is a native of Charleston and resides in Mount Pleasant. In addition to a lengthy career in medical product development, Dr. Horres served for twenty-five years as an adjunct associate professor of cell biology at Duke University, where he was involved in cardiac research and teaching. He holds twelve U.S. patents and has forty-four publications in his field. He has been listed in *American Men and Women of Science*, *Who's Who in Science and Engineering*, *Who's Who in the West* and *Who's Who in Emerging Leaders*. Other published works include two articles on Charleston's Civil War history in the *South Carolina Historical Magazine* and a children's book on the history of Fort Sumter, *Jack the Cat that Went to War*.

Dr. Horres has been a volunteer researcher and interpretive guide for the National Park Service since 2001. His work with the National Park Service has led to the discovery of long-lost records of the construction of Fort Sumter and was featured in an exhibit of how the National Park Service uses the National Archives to preserve history. He worked as a developmental history consultant on a historical structure report for Fort Sumter. As part of a National Park Service award-winning program to introduce South Carolina students to the history of Morris Island, Dr. Horres helped lead over thirty field trips to the island. He has also volunteered as a historian for Fort Johnson and has given a number of lectures and guided tours on the history of the site. In 2011, he was invited to lecture on his research on Fort Sumter's construction as part of the Charleston Museum Sesquicentennial Lecture Series.

In 2006, Dr. Horres helped found the African American Historical Alliance to commemorate and preserve our shared legacy, and he served as secretary/treasurer of the organization until 2017. The organization's primary focus was on increasing public awareness of African American Civil War history in South Carolina. During his tenure, the alliance erected a number of monuments to African American heroes of the Civil War and was recognized by the South Carolina African American Heritage Commission for its pioneering work.

Dr. Horres has had a long-standing interest in educating youth in the Charleston area. From 2007 to 2009, he served as chairman of the board of the Bridge of Hope Learning Center, an after-school reading program in partnership with Matilda Dunston Elementary School in North Charleston. He has been a supporter of the University School of the Lowcountry's Learning Outside of the Class program for many years. He helps introduce students to the history of the Lowcountry by providing contextual presentations on slavery and the plantation system and on the history of Fort Sumter and Fort Moultrie. He is currently chairman of the board of directors for the school and has been involved in helping students at the school with career exploration.